INNER VOICES.

A Collection Of Teen Poetry

Edited By Sarah Washer

First published in Great Britain in 2017 by:

YoungWriters

Coltsfoot Drive
Peterborough
PE2 9BF
Telephone: 01733 890066
Website: www.youngwriters.co.uk

All Rights Reserved
Book Design by Ashley Janson
© Copyright Contributors 2017
SB ISBN 978-1-78624-910-4
Printed and bound in the UK by BookPrintingUK
Website: www.bookprintinguk.com
YB0304C

Foreword

Welcome Reader,

Few periods in life are more crucial in human development than in the teenage years. The struggles and trials faced daily can shape and mould our developing persona as we take a tentative step towards our early adult lives. The 'Teen Poets' series aims to bring these growing tribulations to light, providing a valuable snapshot into the thoughts and poetic visions of the teenage mind.

Inner Voices offers a selection of these poems, which were chosen for publication based on style, expression, imagination and technical skill. The result is this entertaining collection full of diverse and imaginative poetry which tackles a range of vital issues whilst also sharing the lighter side of teenage life. Using poetry as their tool, the young writers have taken this opportunity to express their thoughts and feelings through verse.

Here at Young Writers our aim is to encourage creativity in the next generation and to inspire a love of the written word, so it's great to get such an amazing response, with some absolutely fantastic poems. I'd like to congratulate all the poets in this anthology, I hope this inspires them to continue with their creative writing.

Sarah Washer

Contents

Independent Entries

Syma Ahmed (14)	1
Jane Ekwunife (14)	2
Amina Tahsin (15)	4
Joy Adeogun (14)	6
Ayesha Parveen (17)	8
Katie Pedley (15)	10
Bryony Streets (15)	12
Freia Morris (14)	14
Benjamin Jacob Garwood (16)	16
Anya Pope (12)	18
Satiya Yaya (14)	20
Katie Triantafilou (14)	23
Lana Masood Ahmed (13)	24
Emily Rebekah Howe	26
Courtney Kourosh Razavi Rezvani (14)	28
Erin Price (14)	30
Aimen Ummay (13)	32
Hufsah Farooq (18)	34
Abigail Wantling (14)	36
Arveen Kaur Graya (17)	37
Rohan Jhanji-Garrood (13)	38
Isaac Powell (12)	40
Kirsty Wattam (14)	41
Khiana L C Robinson (18)	42
Sandra Benny (15)	44
Ambali Gupta (16)	45
Orla Sims (15)	46
Alix Wellings	47
Cara Sullivan	48
Maddi Davis (12)	49
Natasha Neill (17)	50
Laura Kerr (17)	51
Iqra Bibi (17)	52
Sarah Tricia Taylor (13)	53
Emma Jones-Gill (18)	54
Kayleigh Bendle-Ryder (17)	55
Riley Ann Beard (13)	56
Freya Kathryn Thorpe Goodyear (15)	58
Lucha Partington Momber (12)	60
Aydaan Kausar (17)	62
Rashidat Bodunrin (18)	63
Sofia Maya Metcalf-Riener (16)	64
Lois Hill (13)	65
Aishpreet Kaur (14)	66
Mishael Masood Ahmed (16)	67
Nadia Roumane (16)	68
Ashwin Sandhu (17)	70
Roya Valerie Alsopp	71
Dina Razban (14)	72
Elle Catherine Donnelly (17)	74
Keira Parker (15)	75
Naomi Parfitt (14)	76
Mitchell Butler (13)	78
Luis Hindman (17)	79
Shrouk Elgamal	80
Ella-Rose Mulcare (16)	81
Jessica Beck (15)	82
Hajera Rahman (16)	83
Holly Leanne Benton (15)	84
Leah Kitteridge (13)	85
Shakira Chowdhury (15)	86
Lulu de Montfort (15)	87
Mitali Chavan (13)	88
Charlotte Jane Martin (15)	89
Rosa-May Bown (14)	90
Okechukwu Atuanya (15)	91
Lucy Rose Barradell (18)	92
Bertie Smart (13)	93

Louise Mary Talbot (16)	94
Jasmin Kandola (16)	95
Sienna Duff (18)	96
Nimisha Venkatesh (13)	97
Jess Birtles (16)	98
Annabella George (15)	99
Mazna Khan (16)	100
Megan Louise Whetstone (13)	101
Holly Wilson (13)	102
Lauren Summer Drane (13)	103
Swati Mishra (13)	104
Izzy Warren (12)	105
Jada Sanyaolu (14)	106
Theo Rogers (16)	107
Maya Diaper (16)	108
Bethan Stephens	109
Taryn Pedler (16)	110
Tahera Parveen (14)	111
Caitlin Harrop (17)	112
Shazia Rahman (15)	113
Sophia Lilley McEntyre (13)	114
Tegh Panesar (16)	115
Emilia Dobrzanska (14)	116
Casey-May Butler (14)	117
Megan Sutcliffe (18)	118
H A Riches (14)	119
Lydia Smith (16)	120
Hope Baxter (15)	121
Bethany Scott-Payne (13)	122
Isha Phillips (13)	123
Molly Emery (15)	124
Asraa Abbud (14)	125
Annick Velleannr Nana (14)	126
Milan Isabella Wood (13)	127
Erin Cooney (13)	128
Tilly Owen (12)	129
Amelia Evans (12)	130
Eve Newman (13)	131
Katie Skinner (17)	132
George Scutt (15)	133
Mya Coco-Bassey (14)	134
Chiana Kelly (12)	135
Saara Hadadj (14)	136
Aditya Athiyarath (13)	137
Aimee Louise Davies (15)	138
Layana Rose Sani (15)	139
Katie Lee Beavers (15)	140
Morgan Ludlow (14)	141
Jessica Michelle Pendleton (14)	142
Aisha Pauline Khan (13)	143
Tia Scammell (16)	144
Melissa Simpson (13)	145
Tayla Alison Schofield (13)	146
Evie Watts (15)	147
Lucy Southwick (15)	148
Sophie-Jane Ann Richards (17)	149
Daniel John Blakemore (10)	150
Patricia Popa (14)	151
Megan Frost (15)	152
Gabriel Jude France (15)	153
Sarah Walsh (15)	154
Grace Smith (10)	155
Abi Slayford (12)	156
Melissa Ann Stuart (13)	157
Max Dedman (13)	158
Max Dedman (13)	159
Kia Howell (15)	160
Atlanta Jade Revill (13)	161
Tasmina Begum (18)	162
Tugba Mya Kaygusuz (15)	163
Nikki Rae Ratcliffe (13)	164
Caitlin McCurdy (16)	165
Hafsa Hussain (13)	166

Brentside High School, London

Benjamin Sparrow (14)	167
Aasia Amein	168
Jason Gajari (13)	170
Sarah Smahi (13)	171
Hannah Lunn	172
Riley Bassoli	173

Cockburn School, Leeds

Rhianna Mae France (15)	174
Jordan Aaron Hardy (14)	176

Culcheth High School, Warrington

Darren Woodward (12)   177

Fullbrook School, Addlestone

Amar Mohammed   178

Ipswich Tuition Centre, Ipswich

Diarmait Finch (13)   179

Luckley House School, Wokingham

Amelie Clarke (11)   180

Samworth Church Academy, Mansfield

Amelia Shackleford (12)   181
Katie Hardwick (15)   182
Ellie Carter (11)   184
Tia Southway (12)   185
Ellie Green (13)   186

Sharp Tutoring, Texas

Laya Kappagantula (13)   187

The Poems

Children Of Palestine

You're hungry now, but that hunger will end,
Your ears are bleeding from the bombs and shots,
Where leaves once danced, shrapnel disperses.
Where children once played, their flesh now searing in ammunition, rotting in the infernal heat,
You're pleading to God, begging him to make it stop - you don't deserve it.
If 9/11 deserved a minute's silence, you deserve for us to never speak again,
You're crying now, well that crying will end.
He knows and he sees your pain,
The shrieks of trauma that rack your brain,
The suffering which scars on the outside, but slaughters on the inside, the soul.
You watched your siblings die, mother and father dead, all a case of martyr.
Your life in a bloodbath will soon conclude,
You'll one day, be among the heavens, in the presence of food.
Bang! One more neighbour gone,
Boom! Slice. Another village obliterated, another handful of innocents dead
Massacre at its finest.
You have met the criteria of 'breathing but not living' – you don't deserve it.
'Oh, people of the world!' you cry, 'Can you not see the horror?'
Things will change soon enough, He knows and He knows best,
The people of the world will listen to your tears,
The howls for help, the screams of terror,
The sound will echo, day in, day out, in their heads until enough is enough,
One day, one day...

Your world is under lock and key, but not for long
One day, Palestine will be free.

Syma Ahmed (14)

The Secret Of Silence

Silence has many secrets.
A secret of a sweet silence is the gentle
breeze of the spring winds flowing from
the north sky. The shimmering silence of
the moon to the roaring thunder of the sun.
The sudden silence of the vast crowd above a
sole player who has won a victory. The silence
of glass before it shatters on the frosty cold
floor, each crisp shard playing its own unique tune.
The silence is found away from the hubbub
of the bundling, bustling city and to the feel-good freshness of the
countryside air.

The sweetness of the first intimate blossom of spring
sprouting in all its goodness. No clouds drifted
in the foamy sea of blue above
nor a single puff of wind ruptured the dazzling
decorations of the sandy dunes of the desert.
Not a sound could be heard either
close at hand or in the far-off distance.
Silence could allow you to hear the twinkly tune of the dense air
Waltzing in the tall broad grass with the old oak
Swaying to the beat ever so slightly.

But silence may not always be sweet for there are
dark silences. The secret of a dark silence
itself can be unnerving.
Become your enemy. The thick, empty silence of a
lover's hand leaving the other shredding them both in two.
The silence of a heart tearing, losing someone so dear. The
piercing silence of a jovial heart that stops
followed by the wails and screams of
the tormented living cocooned by the absolute quiet.

Silence gnaws at your innocent insides. Silence
hung in the air like a rancid smell.
The silence was like a gaping void,
needing to be filled with sounds, words.
Silence was poisonous in
its nothingness, cruelly underscoring how
vapid something has become.
It glides through a room like a silent killer
awaiting its next opponent who would dare to try and break it.

Silence
was just as natural as a dawn devoid
of birdsong. It slyly seeps into every
hollow pore, like a poison slowly paralysing
them from god-given speech.
Is this happening to us?

Unavoidable nothingness. A quiet that is deafening.
The eloquent expression of the inexpressible.
A lonely, constant companion ready to make an entrance
whenever it pleases and when it leaves;
(pause) remains a figure of enigma to us all.

It runs through us, it takes charge in a bat of an eyelid.
We don't even see it coming. It can be sweet;
gentle, a friend by our side but
it can be dark, dangerous, an enemy waiting to strike.
And as I look upon you all today in the humbleness of who I am,
I bid you a solemn thank you
for allowing your silence to speak
when your confined words can't.

Jane Ekwunife (14)

When I Close My Eyes

When I close my eyes...
When I close my eyes I hear...
I hear the wailing sirens that struck fear into the panicking civilians
I hear the fatal explosions that never once failed to murder millions
I hear the bombs bursting and leaving behind only a shadow of what this country used to be
I hear the crackle of the machine guns but I wasn't being pointed at, I was aiming, it was me
It was me

When my eyes are open I hear...
I hear the chirping of the birds that sit on the window sill
I hear the silence of my home that stands ever so still
I hear the ticking of the clock, *tick-tock, tick-tock,*
I hear the clattering of dishes, that gave me a shock

When I close my eyes I see...
I see bullets whistling by taking out the innocent
I see soldiers with grins that prove that they are ignorant
I see a thick cloud of intoxicating smoke curling into the sky
like a cobra searching for prey
I see the injured civilian with molten red blood splashing from their gaping wound
as they wail and slowly turn grey
I didn't mean to pull the trigger but I did
It was me

When my eyes are open I see...
I see a clear blue sky that doesn't fill people with fear
I see fresh green grass that doesn't see a single tear
I see people that are happy
They are not me, they don't see what I see

When I close my eyes I feel...
I feel fearful as my military uniform is drenched with the blood of another
And I'm trembling slightly due to the lifeless body of my friend,
who lay there stained with dried, deadly black blood

I feel terror-stricken as I can still taste the overwhelming scent of death
and the smell of the dried blood burning my nostrils
I feel regretful after seeing innocent people have their dignity stolen away
as they cower in front of the man with the gun
I was the man with the gun
It was me

When my eyes are open I am hit with a painful bang of guilt
When I close my eyes I am hit with the same painful bang of guilt.

Amina Tahsin (15)

A Letter To Oneself

To you, I gift a sad letter
Of a name with no dignity or identity.
A name without the blissful harmony
Belonging to the sonnet that would accompany it.
But a name alone and solitary.

What is your perception of me in a fallacious reality?
Where we are brainwashed into the belief of perfection.
A society where we are deep-seated into becoming social clones
Do not break free from the cage I use to confine you
The prison which strips you bare and leaves you lost.

This is my letter to you about your virtue
Which is as insignificant as a drop in the ocean.
You are no one except the parroted words and phrases
Stating who you are and moulding you into shape
In the end, you really are no one, a mere fabrication of originality.

'Who am I?'

Bedlam rages within your body and yourself
Your head crescendoing choruses of piercing questions
You are a baby, trying to be soothed and rocked to tranquillity
But this is an unbearable state of insanity
The question burns, overwhelming you with flames.

'Who am I?'

I am... the label
Gay, fat, ugly, geek, dork, nerd
The label which has been hammered into our backs
The label, my friend
Whom I must drag aimlessly in hope of redemption.

How can I know who I am if you stifle me with your versions of existence?
If your ideals are as flawed as the dream of Utopia?
And my ideals are deemed idiotic, a joke
Yet the joke is not funny. It's never funny
It's the plea of a victim doing the audacious act of speaking out.

The curse of perfection is plagued among us
Like a still, silent, creeping and deadly epidemic
The cure is the belief that such standards are untrue
My letter isn't romantic, soft or beautiful
It is raw and wholesome, from me to you.

Joy Adeogun (14)

Overthinking Is My Work Of Art

I closed my eyes and I pictured a place where home could be
But the four walls didn't match the image in my frontal lobe
Neither did my heart feel the sense of comfort it so badly craved for
The whiteness of the ceiling simply didn't match the purity it should be
And God knows how hard I tried to create the image into a reality.
I fell in love with the idea
(and that is how I know I'm doomed from the start).

I closed my eyes and imagined how we would grow old together
But our words were just as blank as an empty piece of paper
Seconds dragged on into years and minutes became endless
Time laughed hysterically, mocking my petty fantasies and
somewhere between the empty talks that's when I realised it's pointless
I fell in love with the idea
(and that is how I know I'm doomed from the start).

I closed my eyes and envisaged a career and a doctorate
But somewhere I misplaced my motivation and my perseverance
Whilst life mocked and time decided to fly by
I only had the image fixated to my pointless eyes
Which eventually blew up into flames but the ashes remained
I fell in love with the idea
(and that is how I know I'm doomed from the start).

I closed my eyes and sought sanctuary in a breathtaking world
I opened my eyes and I was surrounded by thorns and spikes
The sky was no longer a beautiful blue and
The birds sang out with screams and shrieks
Everyone and everything ripped my bones apart
I fell in love with the idea
(and that is how I know I'm doomed from the start).

I closed my eyes and thought of nothing
In hope of stopping my mind of contaminating so-called reality
But all I felt was an awful lot of emptiness
Because thinking of nothing is still thinking

And that's the last time I tried to outsmart myself
As my subconscious smirked on it's throne
I fell in love with the idea
(and that is how I know I'm doomed from the start).

Ayesha Parveen (17)

What Do Words Mean?

What more do words say? What more do words mean?
Than a cry in the night that no one ever sees
A cry in the night that no one ever hears
Does anyone listen to the sound of words' tears?
A pitter-patter of rain from the sky
As the words of my mind slowly shrivel and die
The life that words lead doesn't mean anything today
Just like they won't tomorrow or like they did yesterday
Words are a cry of understanding and discontent
They are the difference between what you mean and what you said
The difference between what you think and what you do
The difference between your actions and you
So next time you think your words don't matter
Look around and see how your words truly clatter
Look at all the people your words will touch
How many lives could change by instead of saying 'not much'
You replied with life and your story and your song
And you began to tell people what was truly wrong
If instead of thinking that your words mean nothing
You spoke up and changed your nothing for something
If you gave your words meaning like the potential in you
Instead thinking about all the things words couldn't do
Your words could build skyscrapers and your thoughts touch the clouds
If only the words weren't stuck in your mouth
You could build up an army of workers and the like
Have your own business at the top of your sights
You could teach and reach and soar higher than the birds
If only your voice could ever be heard
So make it and break it and throw it away too
But don't ever give up on the things that words do
Don't be afraid of what could or what might
Just know that the end is never far out of sight
That in the end your voice is yours

Not his or mine or society's to own
It is your voice and your words and your song
That will always reach out and show you where you really belong.

Katie Pedley (15)

Blissful Innocence

Side by side, legs swinging.
Toes grazing the dewy grass as
the wind caresses our bare legs, shyly.
Shifting against the rough wooden seat
we sit a moment longer, waiting?

A hand edging slowly closer;
awkward, staggered movements.
Along muslin first, now knotted wood.
A pause, a deep breath.
My hand lingers, white against willow.

A sideways glance, hoping.
Does he? Doesn't he?
Hand itching, inching still closer.
Silence thrumming between us,
is it uncomfortable? I do not know.

One finger tapping incessantly against my thigh,
and still the silence hangs, struggling.
Something unsaid, unspoken, lingering.
Broken breaths and whispering leaves
left to fill the noiseless cavity instead.

My hand once more begins to creep.
Over the hard ridges of the seat,
across the swollen wood, stealthily.
A naive innocence in the way the fingers splay.

Then I am there.
My hand, an innocent, over his.
I can feel the angles of his bones beneath
my palm, and the tautness of
the skin against his knuckles.

Turning, I see his smile.
Our hands, still one together,
we jump.
And over the grass we scamper,
barefoot in the morning sun.

Free, we skip,
our hands all the while entwined.
The sun growing lower and the day slowly fading.
I place a kiss upon his cheek, farewell.

We share smiles before
our hands part,
dropped back to our sides.
Then he is gone, and my heart is gone with him.

Oh, how natural, how inexperienced a touch.
There is no sin in guilelessness, no crime.
A glimpse of childish first love,
unveiled, untainted, pure.

A life before life of childish fantasy,
of make-believe and stories.
Oh, how effortless it seemed to us back then.
And I wonder now, what of that time
when such a gesture was enough?

Bryony Streets (15)

When I Was A Kid

When I was a kid,
The trees were giants,
The floor was lava,
And the clouds were cotton candy.

I'd dress up,
Fight dragons,
Talk to imaginary friends,
And go exploring.

I used to think, *I wonder what it's like to be big?*

When I was a kid,
I'd get excited about loose teeth,
I'd leave milk and cookies out for Santa,
And I'd squeal at the mention of the Easter bunny.

I wouldn't go to bed when it was bedtime,
I would always have too much energy to sleep,
I'd refuse to eat my greens,
And whine about not being able to watch TV.

Yet I wanted to grow up.

Now the trees are just trees,
The floor is a normal floor,
And the clouds are just that; clouds.

My 'dress-up' is now school uniform,
The dragons have long since gone,
My imaginary friends have left,
And exploring is for 'little kids'.

What happened to me?

I don't have loose teeth,
Santa passed his job on to my parents,
And the Easter bunny's long since retired.

I don't have a bedtime,
I have no energy,
I barely watch TV,
But I still refuse to eat my greens.

I guess I grew up...

If someone asked me what I wanted for my future,
I would simply reply with, 'I don't know.'

And I don't.
But, for a peculiar reason, I find myself longing for the old days.

The days where I would be picked up and spun around,
When I wasn't stressed out over homework,
When I would giggle over the slightest thing,
And when I would smear chocolate cake all over my little face.

I find myself longing for my childhood.
A past, that no matter how hard I try to make it,
Will never come into my future.

Freia Morris (14)

House On The Tides (Sestina)

When the bricks start to break and your foundations crumble,
I'll hold you back from the raging sea.
With all my strength I'll keep you up,
Let me fall under to keep you safe.
I am the rock under your foot,
Try to control me and I'll watch you break.

I still long to see you - it's not only rock that can break,
My heart without you does crumble.
So I stay bound at your foot,
Looking out to the nearing sea.
I'll still try to keep you safe,
Even when things aren't looking up.

All you do is sit when I try to stand you up,
My weakened arms need a break.
Nobody is safe,
I should just let you crumble.
Laughing as you fall into the sea,
Whilst I'm crushed underfoot.

Weakened base slips under restless foot,
Now who's left to keep you up?
Left to drown - lonely - in the sea,
Watching you and your throne break.
Unsupported, you start to crumble,
You need me now you're not safe.

Half the king comes crashing down, thinking he was safe,
The other half merely balances on one foot.
Your foundation falters like a hot apple crumble,
The sky turns black and downturned leaves look up.
Don't stop to watch me break,
I've already been fixed by the sea.

I'm leaving with the current and the waves of the sea,
Forget about me - I don't need you to be safe.
Although your complexion is broken - your soul will never break,
Walk on my love and let the waves guide your foot.
Hold your cracked head high up,
Drop our past and let it crumble.

Let the sea wash you away - just as you let me crumble.
I'll still be looking up at our spot - remember feeling safe?
Spending life under your foot would make anyone break.

Benjamin Jacob Garwood (16)

Anxious

Footsteps echo as I walk to the looming stage, I can see the lone microphone,
I reach for it, and my trembling fingers curl cautiously around the handle,
A rattling breath stutters out of my mouth, and I look to the faces of the audience,

Then I stop, and stare, and scream inside,
It dawns on me suddenly, the sheer amount of people watching and judging me,
Hundreds of unseeing eyes and blank expressions face me. I gulp nervously,

I try to speak, but the words don't come out,
I try to breathe, but the air catches in my throat,
I try to move, but my feet are glued to the floor,

Anxiety glides to the stage and grips my body, shaking me violently,
It swoops inside of me, and holds my hammering heart in its tiny fist,
It has power of my mind and body, and I have no control,

Panic spreads like a winter frost around my body, ice crawling down my limbs.
While my body is stationary my busy mind is roaming wildly,
Toxic thoughts flutter angrily around my head, like small birds trapped in a cage,

But then I replace the frost with a summer breeze, and my body begins to thaw,
I quieten my mind and focus instead on the dust floating through the humid air,
And I release my thoughts from their cage and they leave my mind in a state of gentle peace,

For the moment, I have banished anxiety from my body,
It may be back today, tomorrow or next week, but it can be fought,
It is an improvement, anything is an improvement when it comes to anxiety,

I take a deep breath and splutter out a shaky sentence,
The words begin to flow, as my confidence grows like a flowering plant,
What was I ever so anxious about?

Anya Pope (12)

Just Respect Me

I know you hate me
But you don't need to abuse me
With words of threat
And fists of anger and rejection
I am well aware of your hatred,
Towards me,
But why break me?
Just respect me as if I was a human
With soul
You don't need to accept me,
But respect me.

Every bright morning,
I awake to my senses,
After witnessing
And hearing
The words of destruction
While the adult beside me shakes me
By questioning my care,
But I keep silent
And seal all the truth
Because I am frightened
Of what will happen,
Because I know you hate me
And see me as a joke,
So, I told you
You don't need to accept me,
But just respect me
For my originality
and difference.

Sting, something is hurting me,
Drop, tears on my lap
Wetting my lap with acidic water
Soaking on my cloth,
Screams of fears
Are all that come out
Of my vulnerable soul
That seal my voice
After the long noises
Of pain,
Seeing an instrument before me
Shows me what to do...
As I close my eyes...
Snap, I realise I cherish my life too much
And so I stop the action
With face of guilt and relief
That my soul
Didn't leave my form.

I know you hate,
But you don't need to abuse me
With words of threat
And fists of anger and rejection
Of what I am,
Can I change my form?
Can I change my originality
My difference?
Can you?
Then if you know the answer,
You don't need to accept me
Treat me with respect,
Treat me as you treat other humans
Because I have a soul
That can be fragile
With attacks of wrong words,
So be careful of what you say

Because that could twist my life from
what I call Paradise,
To Hell.

Satiya Yaya (14)

Being Human

I am what God made me to be
Or the accident of insanity
I am the sweetness of a child's first laugh
The breath that escapes her lips for the last time
I am the sound of her deafening sobs as she weeps before his grave
My feet are the earth within which our brothers lay
I am the sound of their screaming as they burn in the fires of Hell so deep
I am Heaven's divine light, shining upon her face as she sleeps
I am stardust, making its way across fathoms of empty space
A single hair on my head embodies the entirety of our race
My arms offer the warmth of a lover's embrace
Yet my hands are drenched in the blood of innocents
My tears are the blood cascading from his chest
The shower of bullets that began his eternal rest
In my eyes I reflect the lights of a thousand cities
Burning with passion across our greatest nations
In the palm of my hand I hold the memories of generations
My heart beats with the vigour of an army drum, marching where others fell
And my booming voice is the essence of falling bombshells
I am the heat of the stars, glowing in their scorching core
I am the sacred secrets hidden behind locked doors
I am death, destroyer of all things
And I am life, maker of beginnings
I am perfection, yet burdened with sin
I am everything yet I am nothing
I am human, laden with faults, yet I shall reign supreme.

Katie Triantafilou (14)

Hidden Passion

Passion... it

Spreads through me like butter
Slicing through me like a cutter
Moulding me into a shape
Stuck together with tape
However, they make me or whatever they say
I will be me
Day after day
Whoever I am and whoever I will be
Wherever I am I will carry on you see
I will charge on ahead and do what I believe
My passion is much stronger than me
So please do not be deceived
And...

I am strong
I am worthy
I am passionate

I believe in peace, equality and right
I don't believe in riots, cruelty or fights
I believe the world will always have some good
And believe this, also really you should
Don't you ever worry
That passion will leave
Or that by it leaving we will be naive
In every heart
There is a part
Of passion that lies
Whatever size
It is kept within
Maybe hidden behind a grin
It could push you further to do unimaginable things

Look at the joy and happiness it brings
Making me want to do more and more
And more
I want to dance 'til I fall
Sing 'til I am hoarse
Write 'til my fingers ache
Express what I think, what I feel, what I see
I want to write a book
Be a president
Make a speech
To change the world
Do something
Be someone
Love pushes me
Fear breaks me
Anger teaches me
Passion drives me
Drives me to my destination
It seems
Of my impossible
Exciting
Unimaginable

Dreams.

Lana Masood Ahmed (13)

That Word

I wake to the sound of rainfall
Mascara crusted in my eyes,
There's lipstick smeared across my face
It's as if I'm trying to smile.
I don't remember much
But I probably had a good time,
I drank too much but that's the usual,
So everything's probably fine.
I do feel a little funny,
My head's running round in circles,
I'm sure it's just a hangover
So honestly, I'm fine.
My skin feels a little itchy,
Maybe it's a reaction to the drugs,
Oh god, there are bruises up my arm
I'm starting to feel numb.
My clothes are on the floor
Tossed far like sweetie wrappers,
I feel too sore to get them,
Well, perhaps, wait no.
Maybe I've been touched.
His lips felt like the antidote to the
Toxins under my tainted skin.
'It's OK,' he said.
I wouldn't feel a thing.
I remember, 'I was asking for it.'
I was showing too much skin,
Oh god, please,
I don't remember a thing. I would have said no,
Surely he wouldn't touch me,
There's just far too much skin.
Please don't say the word.
It was probably just a one night thing.
But that isn't me, but neither is this.
I've been touched.

And I know it.
'You're asking for it, you dirty s***.'
Come on, sweetie, just give in.'
He touched me.
He touched me,
But just please don't use the word,
Please don't say that word.

Emily Rebekah Howe

Tarah Year 9

Goodbye sorry subjects
You can't haunt me no more
No DT to make me hurt
No art to make me snore

I now live a school chapter
Away from geography's Earth ends
No ICT, no RE
No more codes or prayers to send

Cooking was a living nightmare
It chased me like a typhoon
Get ready Courtney, your fate is sealed
It's almost Wednesday afternoon

What could go wrong, I hear you ask?
What dangers could there be?
Setting the school afire, putting glass on the hob
Or losing a finger or three!

Art was a pain in the bum
And a pain in the right hand too
I've never really had a rhythm
With paint, pencil, or glue

And the history of painters was such a bore
Who cares about Van Gogh or Michelangelo?
And I don't care about Picasso, Pollock
Or Leonardo DiCaprio

IT was such a brain buster
I couldn't make head nor tail
I'd spend half an hour writing laborious codes
But if the first word's wrong - such an epic fail!

Python, coding
Bar charts, graphs and pies
No wonder I spent those 60 minutes
Rolling my eyes

I shall offer no blandishment to RE
I never understood Moses or Ali Baba
How did Abraham have a baby so late?
Why was Jesus Christ a superstar?

Hindus, Christians, Muslims, Jews
I honestly respect all
Spanish, triple science
And performing arts I chose
I'm exhilarated
With all of those

So forget about the past, Year 10's on the way
And it's time for GCSE heaven
But where did all this revision come from?
Please can I go back to Year 7!

Courtney Kourosh Razavi Rezvani (14)

A Cry For Help

I've been trying to tell you,
But I can't find the words.
How can I say what's wrong,
When I don't know what's going on?
I'm fighting this war but it's inside my head,
I'm all on my own but I can't carry on.
I need you to understand,
I need you to help.
It's hard to explain but sometimes I feel,
That I'm not really here and the world isn't real.

Suddenly it happens,
I can't breathe, can't think.
My eyes start to blur
And tears escape and roll down my cheeks
And my stomach is lurching, over and over
And I'm sinking down, deeper and deeper
And I'm thrashing around trying to break free,
From this invisible hold that's strangling me
And I'm drowning and gulping and gasping for air,
Pleading for help but nobody's there.
Hands claw at my throat as I try to break free,
From this iron fist that's throttling me.
My pleas turn to cries as my lungs are filled up,
But nobody notices and nobody sees.
Help me! Help me!
Help me, please!

Silence.
No acknowledgement of sorts.
My cries were silent to all nearby ears,
Some people glance but nobody hears.

I never realised that having a voice,
Meant that whether anyone listened wasn't my choice.

But you had to look closely to notice my pain,
For my cries were encrypted, too hard to explain.

Erin Price (14)

Wedding Day

After several months of contemplation
This special day has come
I gaze at my dress in admiration
And on the side, crying, is my mum

Quickly sort out my hair
I look like a total mess
As I sit on a nearby chair
I put on my wedding dress

Hours later I'm finally done
And Dad helps me into the car
Everyone promises lots of fun
And everything's going well so far

As I walk into the hall
I squeeze my dad's hand
I can see my Romeo standing tall
Looking nervous and grand

Uncountable eyes are gazing at me
My cheeks turn hot and rosy-red
I feel like a drop of water in a big sea
On my face several tears have shed

My dad tells him in the ear
'Love her like there's no tomorrow'
On my face slides another tear
As my dad ambles away from me in sorrow

My groom and I sit together
We look happily into each other's eyes
Our love will surely last forever
And on the left my mother cries

Food is served and we excitedly tuck in
We cut the cake and get fed a slice
Now I've got cream on my chin
Everyone says it's really nice

Two hours later the ceremony ends
The pictures have all been taken
Now I'm hugging all my best friends
With my husband I'll never be forsaken

I get in the car with my in-laws
Outside my family waves goodbye
I wonder what my future has in store
As I gaze into the beautiful sky

Oh, what an amazing 'Wedding Day'...

Aimen Ummay (13)

No One's Falling For The Sugar-Coat...

You can say whatever you want
Disguise it however you wish
Pretend, play around, put on a show
Smooth it over with your lies
But I won't fall for the trick
Keep the falsehood coming
I can't wait to see your plan at work
I'm eager over here, in waiting
To point out the mistakes
Uproot your plans
Unmask and unveil
The truth hidden behind your guilty hands
The sweet coat of sugar-coating
The paint over the evil, harsh words
The works
All just plotting in the hidden depths
Fooling everyone
'It's all out of love
Family bonds
Ties of care and friendship
No secrets, no plots'
But I'll drag you out into the open
Let it free
For all and everyone to see
That you're not as sweet as you pretend to be

A rock, a cold-hearted stone
Disappointment, betrayal
Lies, lies, lies
There's no rainbow hidden in the clouds
No sun there, way up high, above
You're just trying to fool everyone
Tricking, plotting, your plans
This sugar-coating, this charade
This mixture of lies and lies

Made to look like colours
Like fun, hope and joy
There's no truth behind your words
No sincerity behind the act
I know
So you should know
That
No one's falling for the sugar-coat.

Hufsah Farooq (18)

Humanity

We stare at our screens 23 hours a day
Hypnotised by the lies that people say
People can fake being happy behind a screen, they can hide an identity
We become a different person, they say it's just creativity
Yet you lose the real you
Off screen or on screen, it's all about if you win or if you lose
What happened to equality and fairness?
There are so many people trying to spread awareness
Yet we all sit here looking at our screens
Slowly saying goodbye to the real world and the fake becomes our reality
We don't realise it, but there are so many casualties
To our own war between ourselves

Will it be too late to find yourself?
Find the real you?
But how can you?
Because there's a thing called expectation
It's a word that needs a long explanation

It's what we see on our screen
What we should have been or what we should be
Change our hair, change our clothes to be the best
But don't you realise, you will just look like all the rest
of humanity because it's just the same
But if you are different, you are apparently 'lame'

People wonder why there are so many wars
Open up your doors
It's because society doesn't accept people to be who they are
And if they are
They are bullied and left with scars...

Abigail Wantling (14)

Hopeless

Why does life always pass us by?
One moment we are four, and then we are nine.
We go from dolls and action figures to pens and paper,
No fun or games, we do not continue to caper.
Why does our childhood get engrossed in education,
All the revision to complete, causes nothing but exasperation.
Why do we assimilate of all the affliction and tribulation in the world not soon enough?
We remain imperceptive to outside happenings.
People think pure innocence is within those that know of no anguish,
But is this not vulnerability, endangerment, in its finest form?
Why do we associate children with purity and as being untainted?
They do not require a filter, but mind they harbour candour which dissipates as they come across the ages,
Their minds, submerged in nothing but falsifications and diffidence.
How did all these years slip out of our fingertips?
There's no time for fallacies, misconceptions, blips.
Why can't we go back in time and restart our lives,
Are we only born to do no more than live to die?
Have we all lost purpose to life?
It seems so apparent, the directionless nature of it.
Do we lose the will to live the more we see the world for what it is?
No longer a fairy tale, no longer a reverie come true
A world full of pessimism,
With people more dreary and disconsolate than you could ever envision.

Arveen Kaur Graya (17)

The Quest Of Tim Bucklau

Bucky lived on Brooks Street,
Next to Stretford Mall,
But there's something about his chromosomes,
He does not have them all.

Sadly now, due to this,
He cannot feel emotion,
But somewhere in the jungle,
There is a secret potion.

He must set off to find it,
So he can be like the rest,
But first he must be equipped,
To set off on his quest.

All Tim took was a small knife,
As that was all he needed,
But all the knife did was provide him with wood,
Because that's all the trees did.

He then made his way through the forest,
And fought through the bracken,
He faced ticks, spiders and leeches,
So he raised his hand and smacked them.

Tim saw many predators,
That lay still and seated,
But Tim was so brave,
When he roared, they retreated.

After many hours fighting through forest,
In the distance he saw the potion,
He could not get excited just yet,
So he lunged at it with mixed emotions.

He grabbed it with his hand,
And drank it with one swallow.
He jumped for joy and smiled widely,
His head was no longer hollow.

He felt his chromosomes grow,
Expanding in his head,
If it wasn't for that day,
He'd probably be dead.

Rohan Jhanji-Garrood (13)

Boy Drowning

Drowning,
He felt great pain, more than he'd ever felt before.
The huge regret of jumping in.
The sorrow that he might never see the light of day again
Or have so much as even a breath.
The water filling inside of him, blocking all possible ways of breathing.
He could not feel the so familiar sensation that was his mother's touch,
Nor the feeling of breathing oxygen through his lungs.

Drowning,
He could hear his friends calling his name, he was just hoping that one of them found him,
He heard the water bubbling after he blew extremely hard, seeking the attention of people passing by,
He heard the muffled scream of a woman who spotted him,
He heard his heart pounding, with panic and devastation,
He couldn't hear the sound of the television that he would be watching if he had stayed in,
He missed the sound of his sister whining for once as well.

Drowning,
He saw a blurred vision of the underwater world,
His house through the stone-cold, transparent ice,
He saw his life flash before his very eyes, wishing it wasn't about to end,
He saw his family in his mind, picturing them all together,
He couldn't see himself surviving this most terrifying experience.
He couldn't see clearly so he closed his eyes and dreamed of Heaven.

Isaac Powell (12)

When No One Notices

Through those open doors she walks, consumed with fear,
Falling from her porcelain-coloured cheek, a tear.
Not wanting to enter the wooden classroom door,
She would rather run or hit the floor.
Never having to live another long day,
Surrounded by looks that make her feel like prey.
At the cruel and malevolent mercy of the hawk
And the others around that glare and gawk.
She must focus on getting through the week,
Even when the horrid melancholy reaches its peak.
At the end of school when she may finally go home,
She must simply sit and wait quietly for the phone.
At last she hears the vibrating sound,
Mocking messages come from the vicious hounds.
She can take no more and must leave this hell,
From the tallest building she jumped and fell.
Who could make her want to take her life?
It was the bully who held the fatal knife.
But they did not physically take her down,
'Cause they knew they could reach her all over town.
The pain had not come from words at school,
But the malicious texts calling her a filthy fool.
For many months this had gone on,
But no one had cared to ask her, 'What's wrong?'
Her teachers and friends never helped her deal
And now at her funeral they do reel.

Kirsty Wattam (14)

Tears In The Eye Of The Beholder

The worst feeling in the world,
Is when I'm minding my own business,
And I hear a ghost of my name.
A skittering whisper not meant for me to register,
A bullet to my chest,
As I suspect,
People are talking about me.
Stomach churning, ears burning,
I try not to listen as,
Hate-seeking missiles are,
Sneakily creeping towards me.
Your aim is always impeccable,
Detecting and wrecking,
The flaws I'm protecting,
Raining on me with your hate until,
Negativity soaks my skin.
I just don't understand why,
You feel the need to point out,
My impurities.
What, you think I don't know?
That I don't have any insecurities?
Too fat, too short, too loud, too brash,
Not dainty enough, not witty enough,
Not sociable enough, not pretty enough,
Well enough is enough!
I am a human being.
I have flaws and faults and I make mistakes,
As does the man over here, the woman over there,
And even you, the one who smirks and glares.
To you I am not perfect, not even close,
But newsflash!
Beauty and perfection are subjective.
A matter of opinion in which
Everyone has their own.

Beauty is in the eye of the beholder,
Well, behold!
They say everyone is prettier with a smile.
Maybe, just maybe,
If we can put this nonsense behind us,
I'll show you mine one day.
Because I like wearing it,
I just wish you'd let me.

Khiana L C Robinson (18)

Puppet Strings

They grasp the strings, so tight,
clutching with a mighty grip
and shut my mouth - shut tight -
the threads piercing my unspoken lips.
The cords snaking over my fluff-filled form,
the ropes choking my free accord
and demanding to sit back, straight, silent solitude, sober.
Their all-dominant hands manoeuvre.
Shift, ploy my corpse-like frame. *Move!*
My lying smile and lying feet and lying hands,
sway and swing with the tear-soaked melody
and the supreme mass of supreme dolls,
thunder-clap my torment and suffering.
They are pleased. I should be...
The constant drumming, the tick-tocking. The voices
Yes, yes, yes, *yes!*
No! I strike the strings, soulless, lifeless, dead.
Alive. The mighty hands unravel. Free.
The strings plummet,
Sinking, sagging, slumping.
The symphonic harmony of a soul, a heart,
ricochet and thunder-roar my waking corpse.
Triumphant, free spirit,
free from the puppet strings.
I dance to the melody of my sorrowful joy,
Swerving, gliding, flying, swaying.
A jewel, a gem, a pearl
of my graceful, pure, elegant finale.
I turn away from the dolls, the hands and
the puppet strings, truthfully
smiling.

Sandra Benny (15)

Young Woman

As I stand here small, yet tall
At 16 years old and watch my mother's silent tears, as she prepares to tell me
The problems a young woman will face,
As she explains how to be careful of the men who grope you using their eyes and evil intentions,
As she tells me late at night I should lower my gaze and cover my shoulders,
For the men await.
As she tells me that people will always use my clothing to explain my sexuality:
Short skirts above my knees,
Obviously equal promiscuity.
To some, though, the long baggy trousers wrapped around my ankles,
Are the forcefully put shackles to contain me?
As my mother tells me, to face the world I must be strong,
My confusion grows further as I think of how I dealt with situations before I had become a young woman
As I dealt with such situations when I was 12 years old and in my school uniform
And felt the eyes of men watch me as I walked home, innocently.
The situation where I was 6, and my big brother walked me to my friend's house,
Yet still, a man whistled at me.
I remember the situation when it was 30 degrees and I couldn't wear shorts to a trip
As my 14-year-old legs would distract the minds of young boys around me.
And sadly I realise, there was no difference; whether a young girl, or a young woman.

Ambali Gupta (16)

The First Thing I Remember About Us

The first thing I remember about us
Was the way you made me smile,
The way you laughed at the things I said, because I said them 'like a child'.
It was the way you would talk, with your voice trying to be low, because even though you were only fourteen, you desperately wanted to grow older.
The way when you brushed a hair from my face, it gave me shudders.
The way we both blushed when we looked at each other.
It was the very first kiss that we ever shared, it was just us, no one was there.
The way we danced, with me in my dress, you in your suit,
Like you were trying to impress!
It was the way when I had to go, you cried so quietly I almost didn't know.
It was the way I cried, when I got the call...
They weren't letting you back into school.
Because of the way you talked in your sleep, or the way you refused to eat.
The way when I came over, your mum would tell me to go.
I was angry with you, because I didn't know.
That you were slowly dying inside...
I was the only thing that made you feel alive...
And though I told you constantly that you were loved,
That didn't seem to be enough.
So, I just want to say I miss you...
And I hope the angels let you have my first memories of you.

Orla Sims (15)

My Feelings

I'm not real, I feel, like this is a dream.
Will I break? I'm not awake, I hate to work in team.
I'm tired, unwired, from all eternity,
Not clever, worst ever, not understanding me.

Not cool, I fall, I have a broken mind.
Irate, no mate, is something you will find.
No friend, dead end, my life is a bore.
Each day, they pray, that I'll be here no more.

Unmapped, I'm trapped, one big mystery.
Gets worse, it hurts, but how bad can it be?
I'm trying, but dying, inside my own head,
Feeing used, confused, I'll just stay in bed.

Unprepared, I'm scared, of what the future holds.
There's tears, and fears, waiting till it unfolds.
Unstable, unable, to feel love or pain.
I'm weird, head cleared, I'm not sure I'm sane.

Can't talk, won't walk, outside my front door.
I try, but cry, and fall down to the floor.
Smash my phone, die alone, no one will be around.
I'll be hated, like everyone's stated, I can't ever be found.

Soul's lost, no cost, it's gone far away.
Can't be seen, I'm mean, they will make me pay.

Alix Wellings

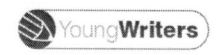

The Dancer

He sits there, blending in:
Another man enjoying the show,
Another man in pin-striped trousers,
Swollen gut spilling over his belt.
He sits and he watches the spectacle,
The girl who moves like a fawn.

A slice of ankle and wrist.
Long, loose hands, gentle arches,
Buttermilk silk and smooth legs,
Supple flesh glowing with peach fuzz,
As static as her locks of honey-blonde.

She bends
And her body pushes through white fabric,
Longing to be gratified, touched -
The dips and peaks of bulging ribs,
Pert nipples like buds yet to blossom.
She flutters, spins, sighs, the strum of her feet
As soft as a butterfly's wing.
Her skin is elastic, pristine, ready to spring back to shape
Like a ripened sponge.

He would be the first, he thinks.
The first to claim her,
Like footprints in fresh snow.

She is a taut, white canvas,
Stretched to perfection, awaiting paint.

His crafted meal of fresh juice and lithe flesh,
Teeming with warmth and served beneath a spotlight,
For all to see his ugly truth,
Her beautiful secrets,
In a flurry of flying roses.

Cara Sullivan

Teenage Years

Darkness, holding me back from where I want to go,
failing me though I want to succeed.
Panicking, out of time, I can't make it.
The words circle my head, such a dark place.
My mind overflows with thoughts, with pain, with anger.
The questions and worries drive me insane,
I'm stuck in my mind with my thoughts.
It's sometimes hard for me,
to see the world how other people see it,
some beautiful place where miracles happen.
People say life has meaning, everyone's born for a reason.
Happiness always comes to an end.
If you go up too high you'll come down even faster,
or at least that's what happened to me.
I was soaring too high, it was nice, I was happy
but then I came down, down to reality.
The truth came so heavily upon me, I couldn't handle it.
It drove me insane, I had no sense of what was real anymore.
It made me think a lot, everything just became thoughts and questions.
I had thought so much, too much.
I had questioned reality, so my reality became my mind.
I dived too deep into my soul,
there was no longer an exit route.
I became my thoughts, I became my questions.
Is staying in my mind the safest way?

Maddi Davis (12)

Slipping Away

I sit here hoping, praying that you last the night,
or, at least, that you wake so we can have our final goodbye
I watch you lying there, you look so small and frail, like a child
I know that death is coming for you and I shed a tear.

I sit here thinking about all the good times we had together,
the times you made me laugh and smile,
the times you held my hand and told me everything was going to be all right.
It is now when you are slipping away that the memories seep back in.
I watch the wall, not wanting to look at you,
knowing that soon I will be in a world where you will not be there.

I sit here wanting to spend every moment with you that I can
I want to be there for you, like you have for me all these years.
I watch the line on the monitor, your heartbeat rise and fall,
wishing that the inevitable doesn't come
but there's no way to stop it.
I know that soon enough the end will come
and you will be gone forever.

I sit and hold your hand as it happens
so fast, so easy.
I am numb, you're gone, you're really gone.
I watch as the line stops, flat, the beeping I can't bear,
I close my eyes and try to go back to a time before you were gone.

I start to cry as I let your hand slip from mine.

Natasha Neill (17)

My Choices

I have a gold, diamond-encrusted goblet,
and yet I choose to drink from a paper cup,
I have water but I choose wine,
shudder when the syrup touches my tongue.
She wants me to be a lady and sit aside,
but I choose to roll around in the dirt.
Give me a candy bar,
or kiss me with your chocolate lips.
I wear our broken records as a necklace,
its shards cut my chest, scoring a constant reminder.
I want you to hold my hand and stroke my wrist,
but instead, you cut them,
and sign your name in the corner, marking your art.
I just want to be left so I can read in the dark,
but your lighter still seems to set my pages on fire,
and burn me in the process.
I wanna see you burn!
Maybe it will mute your heartless words.
I can burn with you if you want?
I left my satin at home.
Just so I could save some rags.
I even polished our picture frame,
Just so you could throw another bottle at it,
then kiss your apologies across my purple neck,
and stick our photograph back together,
with its cracks showing prominently through.
Let's cuddle like lovers,
I'll stitch a smile to my face,
And use the satin to wipe the blood from my mouth.
I chose a knife.
When there were flowers growing at my feet.

Laura Kerr (17)

Actuality

Within my cranium an ancient epic lies,
I battle my mind over the simplest of tasks.

I could work hard but cease functionality,
Instead I devote my invaluable time to thinking of pick-up lines never to be used,
Watching Vines and YouTube.

I swore I'd graduate Cambridge with Masters; the years long gone,
Now I haunt the sixth form halls, lifeless eyes wandering into nothingness.

I'm exhausted, anaemic, asthmatic, an apathetic entity scarred from past relationships rendered mentally traumatised.
Santa is not real. Nor the Tooth Faerie or the Easter Bunny.

There is no Bogeyman to take me in the night,
Just the echo of a nation's wishes, screaming for change.

Dreams of awakening and living a life I once craved are groundless; a reverie.
Feelings rot sour, as footprints of gushing springs tattoo the surface of Mars.

Half-one on the clock, lessons live on -
An interminable cycle, the waves immerse my corpse.

I'm reaching out, holding on for my soul -
You can't take me yet Grim Reaper.

My word ploughs forward.
The frost which chases flames to exile.

Though I may not look it;
I'm breathing,
I'm alive.

Iqra Bibi (17)

Roald Dahl Poem

Willy Wonka owns 'The Chocolate Factory'
He is an amazing treats-maker
and super, mind-blowing inventor
he would create wonderful flavours
the legendary sweets and wonderful treats
were always in the papers

Matilda Wormwood was an average girl
with extraordinary gifts.
When she got mad, especially with her dad, things would shake and lift.
Matilda Wormwood loved to read, she would go to the library
as much she was clever her dad would show displeasure, with every good deed
The reason being, her dad was shady and crooked as they come
Dodgy-dealing and cars where the rule of his thumb

Mr and Mrs Twit were a troublesome pair
always playing pranks here and there
If it wasn't Mrs Twit with her glass eye
it was Mr Twit with the dirty hair he called a beard.
The foolish duo always loved to prank one another
always planning their undercover plots.

He is amazing, fantastic and awesome
that Mr Fox is, I tell ya
so sneaky and cunning
always tricking them farmers
Boggis, Bunce, and Bean are like llamas
so slow to realise things until seconds, minutes or even days later.

Sarah Tricia Taylor (13)

Three Years Too Late

You silently abandoned me without a single word
During three secluded years nothing had I heard
Then quite randomly from you, I receive a text
Three years too late...

Am I meant to be impressed?
No offered apologies or words of explanation
Nor feelings of regret for three years' deprivation
Now you tell me you love me
And that you made a dreadful mistake
Yet to rectify this wrong
A text is the only action you can take?

Three years of lonely Valentines have gone
Did you send a bouquet, card or a single red rose?
No, not a flippin' one!
All I get is a text inviting me for a drink
A little more diligence my dear
Long overdue I think!

Three more birthdays have passed
Making me older and more wise
A gesture other than a text is required
How could you not realise?
Why now after three years' absence
Do you want to see me again?
A question I keep texting you back
The answer to which,
I'm still struggling to attain.

Since we parted there's been no other
'Likewise'
You defensively reciprocate...
So why now, finally, do you choose to contact me
When it's three bloody years too late!

Emma Jones-Gill (18)

It'll Be Okay

It'll be okay
You're going to be fine, my dear
I know it may seem dark now, but in the end it will all become so clear
You'll see
One day you'll find what you're looking for. Once and for all
All this pain you're going through now will make you stronger and you will no longer fall
You will be able to get back up, and shake it all off
Like a gasp for fresh air, you'll be able to breathe freely
When you see, everything's meant to be
You'll start to see that there's a place for you on this Earth

I've once been there myself, the sharp edge seeping its way in
The deeper it gets, the less you win
You spill out everything from the inside
And yes, there's always someone that makes it worth the ride
You feel like they're gonna chew up your words, spit them out like it means nothing
Then you realise that they'll do anything to keep you happy

One day you'll see that life is always meant to be lived by you and me
I can see the spark of hope in your eyes, you just have to believe it
Let me show you.
You're more than worth it!

Kayleigh Bendle-Ryder (17)

Teen Poem

Teens, teens,
So misunderstood,
We bottle up our problems,
And they haunt our childhood.

Teens, teens,
Adults tell us to run the show,
But how can we do that,
When they won't even let us go?

Teens, teens,
We do the best we can,
So please don't tell us to restart,
We're not all Superman.

Teens, teens,
Oh, so pressurised,
Why can't they, for once,
Just let it slide?

Teens, teens,
There is something we all lack,
A necessity of life called sleep,
And we cannot just bounce back.

Teens, teens,
The most indecisive age group you will ever see,
But, really, it's not our fault,
Sometimes, we just can't agree.

Teens, teens,
'You're not an adult.' 'You're not a kid.'
They tell us this, but really,
Who will be the one to outbid?

Teens, teens,
We may seem emotional,
But in reality,
It's uncontrollable.

Teens, teens,
They ask us what we dream,
And what we wish to be,
But not everyone has decided their team,
So just let us be free.

Riley Ann Beard (13)

Stories In The Park

You see that lady over there?
The one with the dog and the reddish-brown hair?
Yeah, that one
Well she's a drug addict
Her face pale,
Crumbling like dried-out mud
Her eyes sunken,
Shot with blood
She tried to give up but it's too hard
So her kids starve
Her dog's insurance hadn't been paid
So she and her loved ones are wasting away
The man over there
The one with the curly moustache and glasses
That's him
Yeah, his mum is dying
Cancer claimed her body
A lump in her bosom,
A lump in her throat,
A lump in her lung
It's terminal,
She going to die
And there's nothing he can do about it
So him and his loved ones are wasting away
See her
The one standing at the edge of the pond?
Yeah, her
Drink has consumed her
She found her daughter hanging
Hanging dead
So she turned to the devil's brew
It takes her rent money
It has her money for food
It consumes her life
So her and her loved ones are wasting away

We are all wasting away
In different ways
We are all inevitably
Wasting away...

Freya Kathryn Thorpe Goodyear (15)

Ever Sleeping Beauty

He stared at her,
His heart breaking, shattering,
Into lots of little pieces.

He stared at her,
His eyes pained, watering,
Trying not to fall apart.

He stared at her,
Her eyes closed, unmoving,
Never changing, never waking up.

He stared at her,
Looking so calm, at peace,
If only she knew she was being betrayed.

He stared at her,
She was so beautiful, exquisite,
If only she knew what he had to do.

He stared at her,
Tears streaming down his cheeks, destroyed,
He didn't bother wiping them away.

He stared at her,
Lifeless yet breathing, a statue,
He loved her too much yet not enough.

He stared at her,
He moved towards her, slowly,
His lips met hers, then he pulled away.

He stared at her,
He pulled his dagger out, defeated,
He hesitated, trying not to break down.

He stared at her,
Her eyes opened, confused,
He plunged the dagger down.

He stared at her,
Her eyes flashed sorrowfully, angrily,
She stopped breathing.

Lucha Partington Momber (12)

Changes

Every jewel seemed to sear its way into my bloodstream.
Sparkles and evidence of glitter were scrubbed away,
Leaving my skin raw and red.
An inch away from expulsion.

Musky scents of fresh outfits,
Pampered costumes,
Caused my stomach to drop and clench tight at the ropes of my heart.
Desperate to hold on,
As to not lose itself.

The back of my eyeballs covered with a tsunami of red,
And the depths of my skull bombarded with the craters of my mind.
Instead of words, I spat out excuses and justified reasoning.
A convulsion of my own spoken English.
An explanation without any explanation.

Pretty pink scarf wrapped around my neck,
Cut from the departed rocks covering the sea bed.
Material that chafed around me causing my breathing to be disturbed.
Somehow I feel it would be better replaced now,
With a beige resistance of strings.

Forcing the mixture of tenuously strained strands,
To cover the drowned parts of my body.
I fail, slumped in a polar opposite mass weight.

Aydaan Kausar (17)

My Silence You See

Cups shaking on the shelves,
Spilt liquid on the floor,
How did this come to be?
An accident, mind intended, thought defeated.
Shutter opens, air floods the room,
The green leaf rises as hope becomes a metaphor of a seed.

Now that cup shaking was tenacious,
You see it was your words that wet my floor.
You sold me pests for my seeds - air deflated room,
And I granted you room in this vacuum,
But alas you breathe inside of me.

Mind surgery has begun,
Gloves, spectacles, my thoughts in work.
May you grant me bail for freedom.
Oh, yes! I am your prisoner,
And here is the justification for my sin;
I was wandering aloof in this darkened room where not the cups you shook could be seen.

Gasp!
I cannot hear you, are you listening to me?
The mind in comatose.
Silence whistles through the room and says to me:
You are me,
You are as blind as I am,
As trapped as I feel,
You create me in silence,
Mind-boggling is it not; the irony
The personification of your mind is me.

Rashidat Bodunrin (18)

Contrite

Like foe and friend, we parted on a sunny June day
the people spoke and were answered
some shouted, 'Hooray,'
others prayed to escape this darkness
whilst I mourned for the partnership that we once had
I grieved for the unity that the future would lack

No more peace
no more friendship
instead divide, hatred and bigotry
once a united nation
now just jumbled-up pieces of three different jigsaw puzzles thrown
carelessly in a discarded old toy box

Our children will not know a world of joy and laughter
rather they will accept the racist slurs and political disaster
to them this terror will be 'normal'
all they will have ever known is this place we call 'the United Kingdom'

I wish we could give them the world they deserve
a world that is secure and safe for everyone
but until this day comes when the world forgets the hate
I will mourn and grieve
giving my apologies to the children a million times

but sorry will never be enough.

Sofia Maya Metcalf-Riener (16)

Dreading The Next Chapter

The moment when you heard the drowning bell,
You knew you'd miss the so-called hell,
You'd been waiting for this moment all your life,
But honestly you don't want to miss the daily strife,
You finally understand what your brother had said,
'Leaving school is what you should dread!'
You reminisce before you say goodbye,
With your heart suddenly wishing it could testify.
But you realise you have to explore,
Otherwise life will become such a bore,
One month later you open the dreaded letter,
Luckily your exam results make you feel so much better,
Fortunately you get straight A*s,
But still can't live happily because of your infinite scars,
There are endless things for you to do,
But you miss your old life and old crew.
Leaving your youth, tore all your friends apart,
So now all you're left with are limited memories, kept safe in your heart.
Soon you will forget the times that you had,
Wishing you never left before it all turned bad.

Lois Hill (13)

Life Of Romeo And Juliet

Romeo a Montague,
A young, passionate man,
He has eyes that are blue
And has the speed of a fan.

Juliet a Capulet,
Young and brave,
Quiet as a mouse
And glows with rave.

Two families against each other,
A secret within,
Between Romeo and Juliet,
They love each other.

Not allowed to marry,
Not allowed to see,
Not allowed to talk,
But on they carry.

Romeo hates Juliet's cousin,
Romeo kills him in a duel,
Romeo has to leave,
Or it would be the end for him.

Juliet is told to marry Paris,
But she refuses.
Then agrees to fake her death
And escape to be with Romeo.

Juliet takes a sleeping potion,
And appears dead,
Romeo doesn't know her plan
And then kills himself.

Juliet eventually wakes up,
Finds her Romeo dead
And also kills herself!

Aishpreet Kaur (14)

Give Me A Clean Slate

Give me a clean slate
Ahead of me I envisage nothing but darkness, an abyss of horror
'A tree with no leaves'
The feelings and emotions inside of me are all scrunched up in a ball, not willing to open up
'A sky with no stars'
I feel like the world has been switched off and only I am left, a lone ranger
'A beach without sand'
Only I am left,
'A shell with no decorations'
I taste the sour taste of disgust in my dry mouth, no one's coming to save me are they?
'A sunset with no inspiration'
I feel the knives penetrating my heart wishing I could rewind time and start over
'An angel with no voice'
Why is this even happening? What made me like this?
'A piano with no sound'
I am nothing but a large emptiness, hole, in this earth
'A world without people'
If only I could undo what has been done and never repeat the actions and sins that have been committed,
'Start over... '

Mishael Masood Ahmed (16)

Alone

Alone.
All I feel is alone.
Consuming my mind, body and senses,
No one realises the tenses,
That I speak in.
That caused this bubble of loneliness,
trapping me from the holiness
of people who could save me
people who could brave me
face me and my smouldering heart
my soldiering part
in my self-deteriorating start.
I need him.
I need him to stop myself from leading a small army into my brain,
causing me pain
letting it rain
with damaging chains,
that would lock me up with my humanity,
causing me vanity,
turning me insane.
He left me,
without a voice,
without a choice,
All I could do was try and function without rejoice.
I couldn't deal
with the sense of hollowness forming in my stomach,
refusing to heal.
Why couldn't it go away?
and stay
in a box zipped up in a far, far corner of my brain.
But no,
I always had to be the one to suffer,
the one to show

that life does not flow
as easily as you want it to.
I was the example,
and you can learn.

Nadia Roumane (16)

Streets Well Worn

I wonder what the rush was rushing to,
Which tired strings were pulled to start it all,
Which rhythm came and humble tune grew,
Why they could not stop to stare and stew,
Why time ran fast when it should crawl.

I wonder whether they saw it true,
Here where rock sprung from hidden source,
Here where sky was bruised with purple hue,
How the pavement cracked and weeks stole through,
How the tarmac rivers ran their course.

I wonder if they saw days long ago,
That was locked in limestone now brittle,
That was wrought in bronze and water below,
Then no one had rushed and life was slow,
Then people saw much, ignored little.

I wonder what the rush was rushing for,
Mind locked away, eyes on the floor,
Feet on the ground and hearts left indoor,
As the rush rushed on with no clue,
I wondered why I was rushing too.

Ashwin Sandhu (17)

The Start Of Something Great

She sits, anxiously waiting, twirling her hair
in contemplation. Are they really that
nice? Does she really look
okay? Will she even recognise them?

He runs, then walks, not wanting to be late nor
puffed out. What would they have to talk
about? Would they forgive him for being
late? How would he know who?

The door opens, another body walks past, the third
in the past five minutes. Closer, closer, is this
it? The butterflies build but no, straight
past. Deep breaths, calm down, composure.

Someone leaves, disgruntled and disappointed, please no,
don't say that's them. Deep breath, open the door,
ready? No. Yes. No. Stop, just keep
walking. Hands must stop sweating, calm down, smile.

He sits down, awkward greetings ensue, wow.
Wow. Coffee, must buy coffee, offer, don't make him
pay. Smile. Smile. Not like that, you're not a
shark. Is it just me, or could this be
The start of something great?

Roya Valerie Alsopp

Just Wait And See

Just wait and see
How wrong you were
And how right I was

Just wait and see
When the lights turn off
The darkness will stay
And the shadows will scoff

Just wait and see
When you're fast asleep
And your nightmares and dreams
Bring out a beast

Just wait and see
When you're all alone
No one will hear
Your silent screams

Just wait and see
How history repeats
No mercy shall be given
To those who plead

Just wait and see
One day it'll come
You'll be watching and praying
For the monsters to be gone

Just wait and see
The headlines would read
What a sudden
Tragedy

Just wait and see
Are you waiting?
Are you watching?
What happens to you
Won't happen to me.

Dina Razban (14)

Dreamcatcher

He goes out to see the dreamcatcher
In his beanie and his scuffed shoes.
It's ten-thirty in the evening
And he's standing on the crooked doorstep
Leaning to reach the shoulder of his loved one.

Dreamcatcher in his right hand,
Heart in his left, the words
Gripped tight between his teeth
But nothing happens next because
He's trying to figure out
How to switch 'I love you' with 'goodbye'.

He must have been standing in the bedroom,
Suitcase in his hand, unaware,
When he heard it - the doorstep creaking
And the tinkle the dreamcatcher
Wasn't making
Because it wasn't there.

No one, including me especially, anymore believes
A promise can be kept,
But I can see what I would miss in leaving -
The way his hair curls under his beanie
As he stands on the crooked doorstep,
The goodbye etched across his forehead;
The cheerful happy mouth
With those mournful words in it.

Elle Catherine Donnelly (17)

Hurting On The Inside

I know you don't feel great,
And I know you are confused,
Your emotions haunt you,
Your fears have caught you
And damaged your soul.
All I want to do is LOL,
But I can't.
With all the mouths moving
In slow motion,
Calling me out
And giving me names,
Calling me stupid
And playing games,
Which hurt a lot more
Than games should feel.
My brain starts to hurt
And my mind stands still.

I know at the moment
You feel broken, coping,
Hoping your life will fall into place,
Let me embrace!
Before I misplace my dignity,
Just because I think differently,
I feel disconnected,
From the world I live in,
Independent, individual,
You have put me down
And made me feel miserable,
I am invisible.
I know you don't feel great,
But I can relate.

Keira Parker (15)

The Four Seasons

Deep thick snow,
The frozen winds that blow,
Icicles hang down,
A frosty winter gown.

Then the green leaves start to grow,
From out of the deep snow,
Melting into pools,
Like small groups of jewels.

As the petals of flowers unfold,
And the beauty of it holds,
The sweet nectar for bees,
And the stem wavers in the cool breeze,

The days get hotter,
Hours become longer,
The sun is high in the sky,
And the ground becomes dry.

The sun beats down,
The coolness of the air drowns,
And the heat of the sun,
Is like the blast of a gun.

But as the days get shorter,
Nearly by a quarter,
The leaves begin to fall,
On the ground they sprawl.

As the harvest begins,
The nightingale sings,
For the ending of the year,
It is close, it is near.

A new year has come,
To see of what we become,
The four seasons come round,
And snow will fall on the ground,

Once again.

Naomi Parfitt (14)

Kids Nowadays

When you see kids nowadays
you can see that they have changed in the last ten years.

Now they smoke, drink and are a nuisance to the elders.
This world has changed.

They talk to their parents like they're nothing
but the mud off the bottom of their shoes.
They ask for everything.
Kids want to stay out until stupid o'clock and that's not right.

Kids nowadays are greedy,
They want everything and if they don't get what they want
they have a tantrum and say the famous line, 'I hate you'
And be unsociable.

In the future I want this to change,
Get rid of the arrogance, selfishness
and make them sociable unlike the kids nowadays,
Make them stop smoking, drinking young
and make them respectable.

Kids nowadays are ignorant!

Mitchell Butler (13)

After You Left

Set your dreams in a forgotten land,
And send your tears where nobody hides.

We are children of the golden age,
Colouring the voids before we kill our creations.

Hide in the light,
And run in the shadows.

Our silhouette is clearer than ever,
But I have lost your ethereal touch.

We trace unsaid thoughts back to their source,
Searching for the moments that vanished.

Lost pictures,
And fading memories.

Set your sails to the forgotten land,
And soar to the distant aura.

We were children of the golden age,
But we've lost the spark in our thoughts.

You left me in this abyss alone,
And promised no return.

But,

Can you change your mind
And build this all again?

Luis Hindman (17)

The Red Rose

You had bought me a rose
A red rose.
A red rose that had just blossomed
A red rose that had just blossomed from within its seed
A red rose that had just blossomed from within its seed and it smelt like love
A red rose that had just blossomed from within its seed and it smelt like love and its petals were held together with forces of passion
A red rose that had just blossomed from within its seed and it smelt like love and its petals were held together with forces of passion but after a few days the forces began to weaken and the petals began to flop
A red rose that had just blossomed from within its seed and it smelt like love and its petals were held together with forces of passion but after a few days the forces began to weaken and the petals began to flop and the smell of love began to fade and the petals began to drop...
And you were gone like the red rose.

Shrouk Elgamal

Hair Today Gone Tomorrow

Dismantled feathers of demolished, knocked-down hair,
A touch of gel hair, a sprinkle of dust there.
Hair and there and everywhere;
All I can sense are the untangled dreadlocks,
Do you have any preferences?
Or are your colours limited stocks?
An imperfect and unbelievable mess,
Pulling out my blonde streaks full of stress.
Hair today, gone tomorrow,
My hair is weeping out of sorrow.
As a star is born,
This hair we shall mourn.
As the barber chops,
My hair unsteadily drops.
Into a mop it goes,
Like a horse's mane touching his toes.
A Grease-styled burnt-out flock,
Tearing the hair away from my forelock.
Hair today, gone tomorrow,
Another Saturday stolen; one we shall borrow.
And as the rising sun goes down,
There's no need to frown.
Chasing us down the road; scissors shall closely follow,
And there will be hair today, gone tomorrow.

Ella-Rose Mulcare (16)

Deceit

Heart filled with desperation,
You tried to inform them of your decison,
We were all terrified,
But it was only you who tried,
To change their wicked,
Unspeakable ways,
But it would seem,
At the moment,
You have failed.
None of us,
Should be forced to endure,
What everyone civilised,
Would generally abhor.
If only we could change the law,
Never again would we be forced to the floor,
Our problem is that you're gradually becoming,
More and more wickedly cunning.
At first we trusted you,
Why wouldn't we?
We believed you were a breath of fresh air,
And then you set fire to our hopes and dreams,
Ignited them as if they were expendable.
How could we have forseen,
What consequences were next in store?
At least we know now,
Never again,
To callously ignore,
Their cries for help -
Next time,
It could be someone else.
Weaker.
Desperate.
Dead.

Jessica Beck (15)

Fools

All guns blazing,
Weapons at hand,
Knives sliced around their waist,
Fastening my loyalty, my pride, my dignity
to my memory;
Dragging angry flashbacks closely behind.

My mind - a black hole, piling in the matter,
absorbing what once was;
Its own - ever so secret - natural disaster.

I march with my army.
Fighting for my country, fighting for my land.

Spilt milk turns to red gallons.
My friends are now my past.
My family; oh my children, my wife!
Are you still alive... waiting for me?
My family; a house of strangers.

My tears are use to no one,
It's my blood they're after.
Fighting to live,
I soldier on.

In the dead of night, waiting to find sleep more than a star,
In the foreign quiet, looking for the source of this peace.

I ask myself, What am I doing?
'Just... fooling about.'

Hajera Rahman (16)

Imperfect

Taunting, is the silent image screaming at me.
An inch out of place.
Unacceptable, a fly-away strand, a blood-red pimple, a tan line.
Never reaching expectations, never belonging.
Imperfect.

The sparkling gold frame.
Oh, what a contrast!
Undeserving.
The magic powder only angers the fierce surface,
Igniting a roaring fire that licks and burns.
Imperfect.

The numbers never lie.
No self-control.
The cloth that insulates us doesn't shrink.
Miraculously! Delusional!
The key to survival must be limited.
Self-discipline is vital.
Imperfect.

What happens when the goal is reached?
The numbers are healthily low,
The glass on the wall is in love and the cloth lasts.
Bragger! Judgemental! Phoney!
Imperfect.

Holly Leanne Benton (15)

Home

Time seemed to pass slower and slower.
Thoughts in my head seemed to get louder and louder.
My life seemed to get worse and worse.

I am abused.
I am invisible.
I am suicidal.

Nobody notices the girl who screams for help.
Nobody notices the girl who is just a little bit too fat.
Nobody notices the girl who comes from a sinister home.

There are lots of fights.
There are lots of drugs.
There are lots of cuts.

It's all the horrible memories.
It's all the failed tests.
It's all the lies that we're told.

It was once okay.
It was once fine
I was once happy.

One day I will be happy.
One day I will be clean.
One day it will come to an end.
One day it will be perfect.

I am running, I need more time.
I have to do something

All it took was one gun.
All it took was one bullet.

Leah Kitteridge (13)

Comatose Patient

How it must seem
To be so lost in thoughts of tranquillity
To pass days and just sit at the window
Look out but never see to the other side
I don't even know what your thoughts would be
If only I could remember
Being newborn and having nothing to do
Just looking up and smiling was enough
Now it isn't
Yet I still need your embrace
To tell me that it will all be OK
But every day when your special visitor comes
They have to tell me that you won't ever see me
Look up and remember me, know me
You will only sit there with your glassy stare
How selfish it seems
That I want you to be well
But only to look after me
It feels like you have abandoned me
Though you sit in the same place where I can find you
You have left me behind on Earth
While your soul drifts away
Further up still
Till you touch what I can only dream of.

Shakira Chowdhury (15)

'Social' Media

When was it our friends turned to followers?
And our follower count became our aim?
When our aims were no longer aspirations
But the number of likes on our Facebook page?

When was it our love turned to likes?
And likes became what mattered most?
When successes stopped being our triumphs
But our most liked Instagram post?

When was it we confused socialising with screens?
And ended up lonelier than ever at night
With no one to hug and no one to love
Just the trivialised power to swipe right.

When was it our success turned to shares?
And our priorities to profile updates?
When we chose Twitter over long deep talks
And started to let Snapchat separate?

Now the only thing holding us together
Is the reasons our minds cannot calm
It's the potent machine driving us apart
That's resting in your palm.

Lulu de Montfort (15)

Human Difference

'A world created, full of different races,
Different people, different views, different colours and faces.
A world so vast, created to share'
But these thoughts are washed away, without a single care.

You view us not as who we are, but by what you see,
For such discrimination, a place, there never should be.
Where we come from and the colours of our skins,
Are all different, all unique, should never be seen as sins.

'No one is born hating another'
So when will we learn to stop judging by colour?
Life is too short and love, too rare,
So set aside your differences and learn to laugh and share.

Create a world free from these plights,
A world without harsh judgements or fights.
Together with people, from many different places,
All different views, colours and faces.

Mitali Chavan (13)

The Doors

The doors, closed.
The darkness, a friend.
The silence, calming before the storm.

Tight spaces trapped my mind and my heart,
Waiting, waiting to be free, to be able to breathe.
The shame of love looming over me,
Making me feel alone.
All I have to do is open the door,
And let the monsters in.

Monsters, magicians, dragons,
Nothing compared to what lies in front of me.
The rejection I shall surely face,
And the looks that will be thrown my way.
This is all so very unfair,
Being made to feel small.

The doors, seem so big,
The darkness, forever weighing down the inevitable.
The silence, scary but gently pushing you to end it.

This is my time,
My time to be who I am.
My time to be alive,
To love like everyone else.
This time I don't stay behind closed doors,
I come out.

Charlotte Jane Martin (15)

This Fire Goes Higher

This fire goes higher,
You said you loved me, you liar.
My situation is dire,
Like a nail in a tyre;
Empty, now deflated,
Your fault. My fault, I hesitated.
This internal riot
May seem quiet
To outsiders
But in my head
It does imbed.
It's loud, too loud.
Bangs, crashes around,
Drowns everything out.
Even the doubt.
No room for anything
But pain.
She reigns
In my brain,
Her broken domain;
Always the same
And always more sane
Than anger.
Sometimes I'm glad to have her.
Anger is livid;
Has no self-control
He has none at all.
With his fire-red hair,
He sits in a chair
Then stands
And paces around.
Whereas sad, with pain, I lounge.

Rosa-May Bown (14)

Criminal

Draw it out. Pull, pull on
Every opportunity
There,
Right underneath the layer of consciousness,
An alternate but similar world exists
I'm alone in this thought.
15 and alive in ways I don't yet understand.
Yes
I dull myself down
Dampen that frightening energy.
Why do I tamper with such strange forces? Am I too different? Too excessive? Unnecessary,
But completely relevant to my destiny; the crazy party for one, that I turn up so hard at.
No wonder I cower when closing my eyelids,
Too afraid to begin thinking of
The possibilities that my unique superpower can unlock.
Love me to sleep - without my guard up.
Nope, not yet. Just watch and sit still.
Let your eyes glaze over, caging your creative criminal.
Convicted for a crime
She did not commit.
Damp, damp, dampen.

Okechukwu Atuanya (15)

Depression

Clouded emotions fill my mind every single day,
There is never anyone around to tell me I will be ok,
At night I go to bed and collapse in a heap,
My body shuts down, but my brain never sleeps,
Instead it's telling me I'm stupid, worthless and dumb,
The world is getting bigger, nowhere to run
Overpowered by hatred, anger and evil,
It's like being possessed by the Devil
Hiding my feelings behind a huge smile,
Allows me to pretend everything is OK for a little while
There goes that demon again, he begins to speak
Calls me ugly, thick and a freak
Then there's that feeling of being all alone,
Like someone's in, but nobody's home
Everything I've done wrong I probably deserved,
I wish I could make all the pain and suffering become reversed.

Lucy Rose Barradell (18)

Pointless Crime

We apologise,
Because even from our eyes,
The world doesn't look good
While we were pretending to be in the hood,
Vandalising stuff,
But it was never enough,
To fill the void inside,
That we were trying to hide,
Our life looked so bleak,
We were only trying to fit into the social clique.

We thought we were cool,
Doing things like messing up the local swimming pool,
Their hard-earned cash,
Destroyed in a hash,
Of spray paint and whispering discussions,
Not thinking of the repercussions,
We were deep in the abyss,
But then it went into a state of dehisce-ence
We realised that whilst we went on with our life,
We didn't notice the strife,
We know this now,
We didn't stop to worry,
And I don't know how,
But dear future generations,
Sorry.

Bertie Smart (13)

Grey

He saw nothing but grey
And as the tears dribbled vigorously down my cheeks,
He simply stared.

He himself was grey,
An inanimate object, he was.
And as a smile fluttered on my face,
He simply looked away in - utter disgrace?

Is that what I was?
A disgrace?
Someone to perhaps misplace?

Once he saw red in me,
Perhaps that's why he 'loved' me.
But he was blue and I was red,
He wasn't so keen on purple, he said.

Though the purple stains on my face,
Although I am a disgrace,
Remain.

But every strong woman claims
'Love is pain',
Therefore I remained
In his plain, grey terrain.

Louise Mary Talbot (16)

My Little Brother
(Dedicated to Simba Dhillon)

I knew this day would eventually come
But never did I know it would come so soon
The news of your departure has broken me
Into small and tiny pieces
I can still picture walking through the doors
To your adorable little face
It was the first time I saw you
The moment we started our journey together
We have come a very long way
From the errands to the park
To the jumps and the laughs
You have always kept me smiling
Though you may leave whilst I am still here I will always feel you near
Now it kills me to say that your journey ends here
I do not understand how it happened so suddenly
But my little brother, just always remember
You'll never be forgotten
I swear...

Jasmin Kandola (16)

Scorpio

Within my majestic eyes, there's a sea of darkness
Shrouded with mystery, a solitary ocean
Rippling waves of intense emotions.
Soft as a blanket yet sharp as blades.
Pursuing passions, through dominance and dynamics.
These eyes, ablaze with burning intensity
Passion, romance and intimacy with a hint of jealousy.
Tread on my tail lightly, never feed me lies,
Your facades are transparent to me
Because I'll peel back layer upon layer of you.
Because my personality presents itself in various shades,
True colours aren't hard to release from their cage and I'll see right through.
I'm a beautiful ocean of secrets
The representation of a water sign
But only those who can handle me,
Can swim exclusively.

Sienna Duff (18)

Rubble

Searching for my dear and beloved,
I am heartbroken.
She is my beautiful daughter, my life,
My one and only token.

I search every single pile,
Hoping this will be the one,
But yet again I'm filled with woe,
Misery, on me, weighs a tonne.

One last rubble, this has to be it,
I slowly surround it, tiptoeing around it.
Dig, I dig, my fingernails bleed with effort.
Finally, I see a twitch and my heart is lit!

Once and for all, I lift her up from all of the rubble,
Her eyes are filled with joy, yet she is too weak to speak.
I cradle her carefully, reassuring her,
Delighted, I am, to hear her coo. I start to weep!

Nimisha Venkatesh (13)

Numb

When the tears roll down your face,
For no apparent reason.
That's numbness.
When you experience so much emotion, hurt and so many thoughts,
That suddenly it turns to nothing.
You feel so much at once that instinctively your body shuts down,
Your humanity switch is off and could be lost, forever.
You look around you at the people you once loved and the world you once thrived in,
With nothing but a blank face and an empty soul.
Happiness is a distant memory,
Which fades with each second of the illusion we call time.
Sitting for hours alone,
Not thinking or feeling, just... existing.
Staring at one spot, hallucinating nothing,
Just a never-ending darkness,
With no hope, no light
No happiness that's in sight.

Jess Birtles (16)

The Monster In My Closet

There's a monster in my closet;
He's tearing my clothes.
I can't tell anyone,
Because nobody knows
There's terror inside of my room at night,
For I'm alone with my closet and the contents it hides.

Every morning I open my closet,
I find the remains,
And I tidy what's left.

The monster sits still,
Gaze piercing my head.
I push him to the back
And face the day with dread.

What if he moves
And sets my clothes on fire?
Will I wash it away
Or just watch in dire?

What if he dies
And I'm left with his corpse?
Will I face the pain
Or shut the closet door?

There's a monster in my closet,
And he never leaves,
Just gets pushed to the back
So he's forever unseen.

Annabella George (15)

Realism

By the time we waste
To how we run from problems in haste.
By our love of wealth
To our fear of the inevitable death.
By the choices we make
To all the opportunities we never take.
And by the way we become life's puppet
In a world that's corrupted.
It indeed suffices to say
All the things we took for granted
Because we thought they weren't what we wanted
Have left this generation empty-handed.
By the way the truth unfolds
That reality is nothing but insanity.
As all too soon society will be our dictator
And nothing will be in our favour.
Revolving around a world
That will become a department of labour.
And with these thoughts I do remain
Dwelling on the fact
That to live in vain is the worst of all pain.

Mazna Khan (16)

Teen Life

Bully me now, bully me later,
Hit me once, shame on you,
Hit me twice, shame on me.
This time shame on me,
As I got determined to grow,
As I thought I was too slow!
While I sparkle in the darkness,
All you think about is trying to be the largest,
While I stand somewhat heartless,
Somehow still being the hardest!
I'm like steel or concrete 'cause I'm the hardest,
Down with a label known to be the largest!
You think you know how it is,
As if it were your daily pop quiz.
You always say, 'Don't worry,
I went through the same experience'
Although how you put it,
I'm sure yours was an inexperience!

Megan Louise Whetstone (13)

Lonely And Scarred

Lying frore, deathlike and alone,
Seems like an affliction I am prone.
Envying all who glide slyly past,
Though experience tells it will not last.

Thoughts unwelcomely start to appear,
Words like daggers drive every fear.
Like a storm-tossed ship, the mind pounds,
Feels like in circles, the bodies go round.

High hopes come crashing down,
From imagining a perfect faraway town.
Letting the fake get under your skin,
Is when the pain, cries and the tears begin.

A face as imperturbable as of any fate,
His only intentions to anger and aggravate.
Each word cuts deeper than the ones before,
Slices confidence like wood and a saw.

Nothing but the impending darkness
Alone.

Holly Wilson (13)

The Sea

The sea, the sea.
So dark and deep.
Where many a sailor drifts off to sleep.
Where fearsome pirates who look for gold,
will search and search until they're old.
Where hypnotic sirens will lure mariners to their death,
and they will sing till their last breath.
Where creatures of the dark, big and small will hide,
beneath the wave where it is cool.

The corpses of men who used to be a slave,
are now lying below in their watery grave.
Where wars and lives are taken and fought on the sea.
So listen, my son, listen closely to me.
If I don't come back from the sea,
then it means I have gone to sleep.

Lauren Summer Drane (13)

My Best Friend

It wasn't long ago that I was another person
I was quiet and shut people out for no reason
I would smile but it wouldn't symbolise happiness
Then one day I met a friend that would soon be my best

She made me happy and opened me up without even knowing
We always had so much fun, it was clear where this friendship was going
When I needed her the most she was always there
We always had so many laughs and cries to share

Every time we talked or laughed the more we would bond
Girl, you know that you always have my shoulder to cry on
If only you knew how important you being my friend means to me
I hope that we are forever 'Manda Bear' and 'Linzi-Bee'.

Swati Mishra (13)

The Door

I knock on the door,
You shut me out,
I don't know anymore,
What it's about.
I just wanted to see you,
Why can't you believe,
What I'm saying? It's true!
I don't want to leave,
But you're making it hard.
If you'd just let me in,
If you'd let down your guard.
Time's wearing thin,
We don't have all day.
If you'd just let me speak,
What I wanted to say.
But I'll come back tomorrow, and I'll visit next week,
In the hope that you'll hear.
I don't want to hurt you,
So there's nothing to fear,
If you ever decide to.

Izzy Warren (12)

The Voices

The voices in my head are confused.
Conflicted.
The child and the adult.
Two people in one.
Two sets of morals
Two sets of priorities
Sparkles and sophistication
Nickelodeon and E4

The choices my mind makes are contradictory
Oxymoronic
Two different decisions
Two opposing resolves

The urges of my body don't coincide
They're clashing
Dance like no one's watching
Lean against the wall and act nonchalant

The voices in my head all come from one brain
I'm on two different wavelengths
Two thought tracks
One me
One teenager.

Jada Sanyaolu (14)

A Mother's Love

Many moons ago when little children slept
By the side of the crib their mothers once kept
Through the night's darkness and in the day's light
Protecting them from harm, keeping them in sight
Yet as time passes on, a crib turns to a bed
No more teddies in arms and no more books are read
Walking out the door with a box of childhood life
Slamming it behind for a day now filled with strife
Yet forgiveness will come as it had for many years
Now lying down beside each other to rid of all fears
For behind the houses' curtains, a mother and son sleep
No matter how old he gets, a mother's love will keep.

Theo Rogers (16)

Is War Really Good?

Is war really good? I've been told again and again that it is
But now I'm standing here next to a body that was his
The empty eyes that now will haunt my dreams
Along with the sound of the other men's screams

Is war really good? The nightmares that it gives you
Those, war, take them back as they're overdue
For now I will never sleep in peace
As I remember the boy that lost his life for me, goodbye Reece

Is war really good? For the things I've seen, I say it is not
Not when you see your friends and family begin to rot
You wish to see even a small smirk from what was your brother
With whom you came to experience war together.

Maya Diaper (16)

Peaceful Night

Melting snow fragranced the breeze
Gliding around like a swarm of bees
Night betrayed the sun
To be hidden when morning began
Retreating so slumber could commence
My dancing wishes would become sense

Darkness raced along the sky
My dreams went on

Hour by hour, my dreams pranced on
Fading slowly, then *boom*, gone
To awake to joyous smiles of the dawn
Undrawing the curtains with a hushed yawn
Light invading the sky
Painting the Earth's ceiling with yellow dye

Sunlight swooped across the sky
My dreams went on
Yes, my dreams went on.

Bethan Stephens

Souled

As her lifeless body wanders the streets,
She cries for her life but no one can see.

Her dress is torn, red blood is splattered,
It's easy to tell a murder has happened.

Her hands are drenched in vile red liquid,
She howls and she screams, her story is wicked.

She weeps and she begs, she can never grow old,
To the Devil, her soul was sold.

Her voice a mere whisper, her words can't escape,
She lets out a blood-curdling scream.

Memories once alive, rush through her mind,
But it's a little too late... as her darkness awaits.

Taryn Pedler (16)

Replaced

Like I had been replaced
Places I was meant to be
Seeing the things I was supposed to see
Only to devise if it were me
But I had been replaced

Like a phantasm of torment
In mental pain of degradation
Just like a restoration
In a desire of restraint
But I had been replaced

Encountering the heaviness of my heart
Carrying the weights on my shoulders
Enduring the convulsion facing me continuously
I went on knowing I had been replaced

As if I was no use, the burden began to grow
The feeling of aggravation deep down in me, so low
The reflection of inadequacy continued to flow
Accepting the replacement, I just continued to go...

Tahera Parveen (14)

I Lit A Candle In The Notre Dame Cathedral

February blossoms a bitter bloom,
Orange robins, pink dahlia flowers;
White ash, washed down with the midday showers
Under roses in an encasing tomb

A eulogy of grace. Poetry looms;
Placed in a bouquet book that lasts only hours
When fading memories dampen and sour,
Now repressed and unable to exhume.

August breaks, reds bleeding in golden waves.
Overseas in the city of love, there
Notre Dame speaks songs of our contentment.

Candle arrays shimmer for all in graves.
Twirling stands of glimmering gold to share,
Each filled with desire and fulfilment.

Caitlin Harrop (17)

The Magic Box

(Inspired by 'Magic Box' by Kit Wright)

I will put in the box,
My album which is as special to me as food and water is to a poor person
And my precious memories which swim around my head every day.

I will put in the box,
My brilliant books which are written by the best authors
And my fabulous, fantastic family who lead me through the right path like a tour guide.

I will put in the box,
Beautiful flowers that open up and release their rich scent
And my friends who are the sun, spreading happiness and light.

I shall look into my box,
At the glistening red sea which shimmers under the bright, yellow sun
And the light blue sky which holds the moon safely at night.

Shazia Rahman (15)

Thirteen Years

A shadow wanders, he is Father Time
When trapped, cornered, I wish it would go fast
However, he is vile, bitter as a lime
Time ticks gradually, the years seem vast
Thirteen years dealing with my parents' strife
Vague emotions blur, I must keep control
They won't interfere as this is my life
Questions die when exhaustion takes its toll
Hesitantly asking stirs greater pain
My valiant efforts would reduce to waste
As knowledge of despair is all I gain
Yet ecstasy is what I itch to taste
Lives may conclusively be free to flow
However, in tragic circles I still go!

Sophia Lilley McEntyre (13)

To Cage A Caterpillar

I am now a butterfly!
Being caged is only a phase in my lifetime so
My potential is infinite because
I can fly with wings for now I know
The cocoon was of my own creation;
It stopped me from believing.
Forged from my doubts and ignorance,
I screamed as I attempted to break the walls of my cell.
For years I was held stagnant and imprisoned so
I lost faith in a chance of freedom because
I was ugly at heart and mind.
By limiting my sight of success,
I didn't foresee a future of welfare
I remembered a past of sorrow
Because I had no wings to soar skies of beauty,
I was a nothing. I was a caterpillar
(Now read from bottom to top).

Tegh Panesar (16)

Music

Turn the music on,
Turn the music on,
So I can escape,
To a world of my own.

Forget the chatter around you,
Forget you're not chic,
Because where the world fails,
The music speaks.

It's not just a song,
It's not just a rhyme,
It's the air that I breathe,
And it saves me all the time.

People will leave you,
They will walk away,
But when everyone goes,
The music will always stay.

Music is life,
Music is love,
May it send a sweet message,
Like a pure white dove.

You can dance to the beat,
And you can always sing along,
But you should know that the words,
Have more meaning than the song.

Emilia Dobrzanska (14)

Ghost Girl

Her long black hair glittered in the moonlight
Her vibrant sapphire eyes sparkled with delight
Her pale skin was bold from the cold
Her features were that of a doll

Her nose was small and narrow
Her eyesight was as sharp as a sparrow
Her fingers were long and thin
Her body shape was lithe and slim

Her smile was as bright as the stars
Her birthday was the 5th of March
An hour-glass figure with large, innocent eyes
She never planned for her demise

For on that fateful night in May...
Death took her soul away.

Casey-May Butler (14)

The Luck Of A Friend

How lucky am I
To have friends such as these?
Friends that hold me close
That won't say goodbye.

Friends that chase away the bad days
That hold me close and whisper,
'Don't worry, my friend, we shall make it through the haze.'

My friends, they make me smile,
They make me laugh,
They make me laugh when all I want to do is cry,
For these wonderful people I would run the extra mile.

Sometimes I think I am alone,
Yet how can I be alone?
You see I have friends,
So I'll always have a home.

Megan Sutcliffe (18)

Novocain

I don't want to be treated like glass,
As if I'm going to break,
Nor do I want to be treated like trash,
As if I'm dispensable or fake,
Even though you disappeared so many years ago,
There is still a part of me,
Somewhere,
That still wants to show,
How much I miss you in every single way.

No amount of medication will make this headache go away,
Not a second that I don't miss you in every single day,
And I somewhat know this won't matter to you now,
But no amount of Novocain,
Will ever be able to numb the pain,
That I have received after losing you.

H A Riches (14)

Battle Wounds

Bruised and battered,
I begin to unfold.
The ripple of my pathway,
And all the memories untold.

But when I tell you I'm torn,
You assume it's my skin,
But darling, it isn't only my flesh,
That's had a war to win.

I flood with unspoken words,
And hazy thoughts,
But only then do I realise,
I analyse the faults.

The cement over my heart,
Was built by every lie said,
And I knew nothing could torture you
More than the 'what ifs' that fled.

Lydia Smith (16)

Fade

I remember how you'd make me laugh or how I'd smile,
when you were there, and frown when you were gone.
But I can't remember your voice, that seemed so strong
and never left me scared and I can't remember how you looked
or that smile which was always there.
It seems almost cruel to think that the thing I want, so dear
is the one thing I can't have and like your scent is gone with the wind...
Slowly you are fading from my mind, slipping away from me.
Even the pictures seem to lose their light as you fade away from me.

Hope Baxter (15)

Life

Sometimes I wonder if we are here for a reason.
Like was that mother meant to have her son?
Were we supposed to meet the people we find?
Were some made to be this kind?

We meet a lot of people in our life.
It was good when the husband met his wife,
But was it good when they fought?
What would that have taught?

People are falling out of love
They just want to be a free dove.
While others make new memories,
Some have to visit cemeteries.

It may be hard to let go
But there is one thing you should know
Life will get better,
Life will get better.

Bethany Scott-Payne (13)

Imagination

My imagination runs wild at night,
My mother always tells me to sleep tight.
I close my eyes and start to dream,
And before you know it I'm off to sleep.
Witches and fairies start swimming through my mind,
I really don't understand what they're trying to find.
I drift away like a boat at sea,
Lost and found, like little Dory.
When the clock strikes midnight,
Cinderella is running through the twilight.
Some nights I wake up in shock:
Maybe I should stop dreaming about warlocks.
Eventually I wake up,
Then suddenly my world speeds up.

Isha Phillips (13)

To Thee

To thee I leave my heart,
And with thee I must depart.
Though the sun may no longer shine
I was yours and you were mine.

To thee I leave my happiness
Which from this point on won't serve a purpose.
My smiles toward you, all but a waste
Then you were gone with such haste.

Finally, to thee I leave my soul,
Battered, bruised, no longer whole.
You caught my attention, captured my mind,
But now you're gone, you left me behind.

I loved you, I thought you loved me.
Why did you take leave so suddenly?

Molly Emery (15)

Dreams

How I live is who I am
I try to show them

I'm not who they make me up to be
Do they believe me, or do they not?

I can't say what I'm feeling now
Only I know the pain I feel inside

I no longer want to hide
I want to be free of their grasp

I want to be who God made me to be
I'm tired of trying to get you to see

How much I love you, you don't know
Someday I will only be a soul or a thought

Not real or existing
But just a girl with a dream that didn't succeed.

Asraa Abbud (14)

It's Life

The world is a scary place
Where everyone is trying to survive.
We all want to live
But we all don't want to die.
Some of us are scared,
Some of us are depressed,
Some of us are even stressed
Our life is a mess.
We feel as though the end is near
Trying to face our fears,
However all we need to know is we are in this together,
We are all equal.
We live in the same world
But we treat each other differently.
We all want the same things
But all we do is fight,
Why is the world like this
When all we want is peace?

Annick Velleannr Nana (14)

The Peculiar Thoughts Of A Stoner

Blazing blue skies,
An endless sea,
Swimming through joyously,
Clouds,
The wispy kind, as white as paper move
On a journey to the moon.

Dry highs,
The idiosyncratic idea of Boston cream pie,
A battlefield filled with butterflies.
Long nights of wild fire,
Stars twinkle like a smile that never reaches the hearts' open doors.

S'mores are burnt now,
Unable to escape the char.
Eyes are beautiful,
Veins showing red,
The bloodstream flows
As melted marshmallows...

Fall to the ground.

Milan Isabella Wood (13)

Remember

I solemnly plodded closer to the oyster-coloured stone
Remembering fighting truths he told in his grieving tone
Of guns, bombs exploding, memories of his own
I used to listen politely in the form shown

He told me of the soldiers, fighting for their lives
Their country
Their people
Their children
Their wives

Now you rest up in the clouds, skin 'n' bone
I place your best flower, the poppy,
On your oyster-coloured stone.

Erin Cooney (13)

The Undiscovered Poet

The undiscovered poet,
Sits there at her desk,
I bet you don't know it,
But she's writing to impress.

Her pen scribbles across the sheet,
As she thinks what to write,
She needs to make it neat,
So her career can fly as high as a kite.

The undiscovered poet,
Writes down what she thinks,
I bet you don't know it,
But she barely even blinks.

Soon, you'll have heard of her name,
But that day is far away,
For it's her life's aim,
To be heard by everyone, one day.

Tilly Owen (12)

Enough Is Enough

You walk into school
Sometimes feeling like a fool
You're the lowest year
With the most fear
Everybody watching
No doubt mocking
Sometimes you feel alone
While bullies sit on a throne
You think if you smile all the time
The world will think you're fine
And think if you surround yourself with friends
That all of this would end
You want to cry
But you have to lie
Your head is always spinning
It means they're still winning
Enough is enough
Don't pretend you're tough.

Amelia Evans (12)

Am I Good Enough Yet?

Am I good enough yet?
All these expectations are making me insane,
All I ever feel now is pain,
Too fat too thin,
Will I ever win?

Am I good enough yet?

Too short too tall,
Spend way too much money at the mall,
Crop tops, skinny jeans,
Expectations are high for teens.

Am I good enough yet?

No one approves of me,
Why does no one look at me?
There's so much more to see
I don't know what to do,
I feel like I just belong in a zoo.

Am I good enough yet?

Eve Newman (13)

I Guess So

I never quite thought
of human existence
and the simple
pleasure it held
like lemonade bubbling
on my lips like a
sweet kiss from him
and nothing quite astounds me
like love does
we define a certain feeling
with a four-letter word
yet this feeling can span
an entire infinite entity
if the right person is found
and our own being
is just a very small impossibility
made real
because our life is so
improbable that we shouldn't be here
I shouldn't be here
but I am
at least
I guess so.

Katie Skinner (17)

Untitled

This remains untitled.
Like many my age. We strive
and yearn for greatness.
We're caught up in the heat,
we never notice the opportunity,
to assert our precocious minds.

Tell me teacher, why do we have
our ABCs? Cat got your tongue?
Do you simply not know?
Absorbed by your hubris, your degree?
I treated you like family, no more.

All I have is myself, an untitled novel
waiting for my pages to be scribed,
waiting for someone to rip me out
and start me over again.

George Scutt (15)

The Pursuit

Empty as if the ocean
decided to run away,
or the blue in the sky
faded out one day,
and all that was left
was dry and grey.
But
I want to be so full
that there's no space at all,
for thoughts of being blue
or having nothing to do,
just put white light
shining right through,
and love of life and you.
So
Let's lure the ocean back home
and paint the sky with me,
because if we colour in the lines
the picture's all we see,
happiness is fiction
so I pursue serenity.

Mya Coco-Bassey (14)

The Slumbering Giant

Bing, bang, whoosh
It roared
As the volcano awoke
Whilst lava poured.

Orange, yellow and red
Flowed down the side
Rocks tumbled
Making way for a lava slide.

Ash began to pour out
It began to fill the sky
It all happened
In a blink of an eye.

Then there was a pause
There was only silence
The giant had fallen asleep
And stopped all his violence.

Chiana Kelly (12)

They Dare Not Look

I am like the ocean so deep,
Secrets and untold mysteries gather beneath
No one dares to look too close
Afraid of what is coming next
They think my fears will swim to the coast
That is why they do not come too close
I am like the ocean so deep
No one looks beyond my gaze
They judge me by their first glance
My treasures unknown to their eyes
My beauty only seen by the Most High
They never look through my layers
Yet they are in search of my unseen treasures.

Saara Hadadj (14)

The Legend Of The Dragon

It is several metres tall,
The head of the beast is in the clouds,
The length of its tail is immeasurable,
And when wielding its tail,
It can demolish castles with barely any effort.
It has millions of multicoloured scales,
Each glimmer with the colours of the rainbow when it is in the sun,
That is the legend of the dragon which once used to roam the lands,
Where London is located,
And some say it is still alive, hiding in the shadows, and craving blood...

Aditya Athiyarath (13)

I Don't Mean To Be Angry

I don't mean to be angry,
I just see red,
It's just hard sometimes,
I do try my best.

I don't mean to be angry,
I just get wound up,
When people call me names,
And make fun of me.

I don't mean to be angry
It's all these emotions,
I don't mean to hit you,
I don't mean to kick you,

I don't mean to be angry,
But you don't listen to the reason why.
I don't mean to be angry
And they are the reasons why.

Aimee Louise Davies (15)

Death's Game

We are the players
Life is the game
Death is the dark horse
Winning again.

Got tricks up his sleeve
A grin on his face,
He pulls a wildcard
As he starts the chase.

Don't look for him
Don't search around
The path is set
You will be found.

And at the ambush,
Don't shed a tear
Don't try to escape
Or show any fear.

Look him in the eye
And put on a smile
Say these wise words,
'Old friend, it's been a while.'

Layana Rose Sani (15)

Beauty

I look around me,
Beauty is what I see,
But sometimes, I can't see it,
My mind needs to be freed.

I know there is beauty,
Everywhere I look,
But sometimes, I can't see it -
Even though it's an open book.

I know there is beauty,
But at the moment,
I can't see.
Will you sit beside me
Until I see,
The beauty in being free
And
Being
Me?

Katie Lee Beavers (15)

To Live

To be 'alone',
- to be by oneself
Yet
Despite the company, I feel withdrawn

To be 'perfect',
- to become what I am not
Yet
All I can be is far less than flawless

To 'live',
- to feature in your own fairy tale
Yet
All I see, is darkness around each corner

And surely, to not be alone is to be perfect,
And to be perfect is to 'live'

But, I am not perfect
But I am alone
Yet

I am still living.

Morgan Ludlow (14)

Caring

If it is for a pet or a person
If it's for an object or thought
If you care for it
Then it must be special

An object or thought can be close to you
A pet or person can be closer
You may care a little
Or care a lot

Your caring is special
Your caring is unique
Your care is yours
Yours to be shared

You don't need to care for just one thing
If you care you care
If you don't you don't
But it is better to care.

Jessica Michelle Pendleton (14)

Anxious

My every action
Overthought, then regretted
Their every stare
Seeping with judgement
My nights spent
Withering and cringing
My every prayer
Wasted over the wish for a time machine
Small dark corners
Suddenly seem so inviting

My laugh met
With awkward silences
My comments shut down
With behind-my-back looks

Constantly worrying what others think
Whether it be what I said -
Or how I think
Whatever I do,
It just feels so wrong...

Aisha Pauline Khan (13)

Don't Wanna

I'm drifting,
Slowly moving to being an adult
But it feels as though my body's resisting
My body's in a revolt
I don't wanna be an adult

I'm growing,
Slowly but surely getting older
Everyone around me is evolving
But I'm stuck beneath a boulder
I don't wanna be older

I'm stuck,
I'm trapped
It's just my luck
I keep running the same track
I don't wanna be trapped.

Tia Scammell (16)

My Heaven

The sun on my skin, the birds flap their wings.
I hear a distant ring of seagulls flying in.
The sand is soft to touch, like the faint smush of a paint brush.
And the setting fitted in, like a dream left fading dim.
I was alone, no phone.
For once I felt 'at home'
The space around me glowed.

So this is what Heaven must be like
Worries flying out my head.
And, maybe then, in that moment I was sure I could be dead.

Melissa Simpson (13)

Negativity

To those who are negative about everything in life,
Here's my question to you:
If you died tomorrow,
Would you be proud of who you once were?
Or would you be full of sorrow
That no one was at your funeral?
So, from now on, don't count the days,
Make the days count.
Be proud of who you are
So, when your day comes,
Your answer to me would be,
I am proud of who I am.

Tayla Alison Schofield (13)

Broken Infatuation

Your blue satin eyes were devastatingly beautiful,
Their glassy exterior resembled delicate pearls encased in lifeless souls.
Lingering memories still remained upon your lips,
Like a fractured replica of yesterday's bittersweet sorrows,
Turning into shards of tragic nostalgia.
Waiting for you was like waiting for a sunrise;
Inexplicable radiance in a world of melancholic darkness.

Evie Watts (15)

Bullied

Please listen to me, I have something to say,
I come to school to learn, not to be bullied
I feel like no one wants to talk to me because I am different
They call me names, I do not even know what they mean.
I sit on my own during break, lunch and lessons and all I want is someone to be my friend.
Someone talk to me if I feel low, someone who I can trust
So please listen to me, I know what you are feeling.

Lucy Southwick (15)

Elements

Maybe I shouldn't be alive.
Maybe just maybe,
And maybe I shouldn't try because,
One day the rain will stop pouring,
The sun will stop shining,
And the wind will be no more.
I was born without rain in the midst of a hurricane.
I built a wall so high that no matter how hard the sun shone it didn't pierce my skin.
I entrenched myself so deep in pain that the hardest wind could not move this burden.

Sophie-Jane Ann Richards (17)

I Can...

I can be happy,
I can be sad,
I can be angry,
I can be mad,

I can be lonely,
I can be confused,
And sometimes it seems
That somebody has just blown my fuse.

I can be clever,
I can be dumb,
I can be hopeless,
I can be fun,

I can be an author,
I can be an athlete,
I can be anything.

Daniel John Blakemore (10)

Growing Older

Stolen innocence;
My disposition humble,
The limbs our instruments,
Will soon crumble

Victims of time
Reeking of regret,
Figure once sublime,
Vanishing silhouette

Dissected hearts lie
Open, ripe for infecting,
Nightmares multiply,
Parasites collecting,

The echo of childhood,
Quiet as a thief,
Discreet is not good,
Features disintegrate from grief.

Patricia Popa (14)

She Writes

She writes wearily to
shut her mind of sorrow,

She writes wearily to
cleanse her heart she gave him,
but only to borrow.

Her eyes scream sadness at them,
hands still sown paper to pen,
but she doesn't care at all.

She could paint a thousand words,
but none of them compared to him,
his hands as fragile as bluebirds,
and lips as soft as sin.

Megan Frost (15)

Left

Left in ruin,
Left in decay,
All is abandoned and we still complain,
Yet it is our fault,
Our creation,
Our own knowledge has destroyed us,
Slowly but surely,
Leaving us in vain,
It's our future that we have made,
Who are we?
Why are we here?
Because all we have done is make things worse.

Gabriel Jude France (15)

The Moth

Unsettled, it dances and
Flutters around the unlit room.
How, an animal so small,
Does it manage to scare so well?
Shivers go down my spine,
Even at the simple sight
Of the insect in flight.
Its existence keeps me from sleep,
Or is it just an excuse?
My focus trained on the insect,
Keeping me from the dark thoughts
That began in the black room.

Sarah Walsh (15)

My Mum

My mum is loving, my mum is kind
Even though she has a big behind

She makes me laugh, she makes me giggle
She loves to dance, she has to wiggle

She cooks me dinner and wishes she was thinner

Her dinners are nice, she tries her best
But at the end of the day, she needs to rest.

Grace Smith (10)

Beach

It comes gushing in,
Waves high and low,
Clear blue water.
Fish swimming around you.
The sand gets in-between your toes.
Sandcastles being built all around you.
The sun is shining,
People sunbathing,
Cocktails being made,
Ice cream being eaten,
People having a good time.

Abi Slayford (12)

Rain

Rain patters softly,
Sliding down the orchid leaves.

Cascading rice grains.

Silently, they fly,
Twirling through the fragrant breeze,
Tumbling to soil.

Dark hair behind her,
Parasol caught in her hand,
Pale skin, coal-black eyes.

Twilight upon her,
Her face illuminated,
By the moon and stars.

Melissa Ann Stuart (13)

Love Light

Out of the gloom,
And out of the dark,
There came a light,
There came a spark.

Light my life,
And flame my fear,
Fire almighty,
Do singe and sear.

And in this life,
Let there be heat,
Bake my bread,
And cook my meat.

Warm the world,
And light the skies,
Let there be fire,
Till the end is nigh.

Max Dedman (13)

Sleep

Sleep in silence,
Sleep in sound.
Sleep so deeply,
And peace is found.

Sleep in darkness,
Sleep in light.
Sleep so tiredly,
And sleep all night.

Sleep on feathers,
Sleep on nails.
Sleep so dreamily,
And dreams your tales.

Max Dedman (13)

Demon In Disguise

I'm falling for your eyes,
but they don't know me yet
and with a feeling I'll forget.
I'll fade away.
into the abyss,
the one you made
and called home.
This feeling.
This trap.
This is not safety,
you are no lady.
but a demon
disguised as a lady.

Kia Howell (15)

Forever And A Day

Things are better
The sun is hotter
The rain is wetter
I can feel again

The wind is stronger
The grass is greener
My cup is half-full
No longer half-empty
No feelings are null
Life isn't dull

I wish it would stay
But it slips away
Day after day.

Atlanta Jade Revill (13)

Insecure

People say looks don't matter,
Please throw that opinion in the gutter,
'Looks can kill'
You need to chill.
Breaking people's confidence,
What do you think you're doing? Gaining dominance?
You're a fool,
Who only knows how to drool.

Tasmina Begum (18)

Heaven Unearthed

Granted was a wind,
Its caustic whisper.
Expelled from their resting,
Sat perched,
Unearthly beings roamed.
And without fail,
Languished woefully.
Fallaciously wrought endeavours,
Ignited the twilight with a latent breeze,
Unseen and unheard.

Tugba Mya Kaygusuz (15)

Time Of Death

Life isn't as good as it seems,
And when you die a beautiful light beams,
An endless clock ticks out your time,
And when your time's up, the clock will chime,
There is no time to say goodbye,
Only to watch above as other people die.

Nikki Rae Ratcliffe (13)

Fading

Her colour has faded,
No stories left to write.
Actions now uptight,
She is to be jaded.

Feelings to be traded,
Nothing other than spite,
Fuels her final fight.
Wounds now to be aided.

Caitlin McCurdy (16)

Environment

R ecycling is,
E nvironmentally friendly so,
C ome join me,
Y ou can make a change,
C hange our future,
L ive,
E nvironmentally friendly.

Hafsa Hussain (13)

Teenage Lies, Pleasant Surprise

'Teenage years are the hardest part of your life,
They're full of fears and full of strife',
That's what our parents always say,
But it turns out, it's actually okay.

'As you go about your day, you'll start to smell,
So in order to stay clean, you mush wash well',
Even if washing regularly is something new,
It's merely another thing each day for us to do.

'You will discover different types of emotion,
Your starting point of adolescence is set in motion',
So what if these feelings are different for you,
It's an important changing point for us to go through.

'Slowly but surely, friendships drift away,
Your friends become strangers that you see every day'.
If a friendship was broken so easily, they're not real friends,
Because in real friendships, people make amends.

These are just some teenage lies,
But it all turns out to be a pleasant surprise.

Benjamin Sparrow (14)
Brentside High School, London

War Child

Everyone praises, salutes and prays for
The soldiers fighting at war.
But somewhere in those damned countries,
Is a family of four.
Mummy had to wear scarves,
And Daddy was taken away.
Dear brother was forced to fight
Leaving little sister to pray.

Oh God, thank you for my life,
My food, water and bed.
But if you can grant a wish,
Please get rid of the Jinn in mummy's head.

Little girl, when it's time to go to sleep,
Don't listen to the screams nearby.
Just close your eyes, do not cry,
And sing yourself a lullaby.
Ignore the bombs from their attack,
And the soldiers armed with guns,
One day, they will go away
And peace will be everyone's.

Oh God, thank you for my sleep,
My night, evening and my day.
But if you can grant me a little wish,
I wish for the soldiers to go away,
So Mummy won't cry anymore
And Daddy will be allowed to stay.

Little girl, when you wake up,
Look past the dust and shells,
Find a little glimpse of hope,
In your, otherwise, hell.
Just remember, dear brother,
Resting miles away,

And although you're not together,
You will be, one day.

Oh God, I know there are people
Who are less fortunate than me,
But if you can grant just one wish,
I wish for my brother's safety.
I know that Daddy has gone,
And that Mummy isn't fine,
But dear brother needs to find me,
In the depths of what used to be Palestine.

But, little girl, do not worry,
Even if there's nothing you can do,
The world will come to its senses
And you'll have a proper life too.
You'll wake up without being scared,
And Daddy will come back home.
While your country restores its beauty
And you, little girl, will no longer be alone.

Little girl, they say the best dreams happen when you're awake,
But I beg you, please don't dream of the day.
For the soldiers will come once again
And make your family pay.
Pay the price of being there,
Pay the price for being poor.
Just accept the consequences of your life
And pay the price of war.

Aasia Amein
Brentside High School, London

Dear Depression

Get out of my head,
Every single day has become a dread,
I hate you like I hate my life,
I guess it has become a strife.

Behind my smiles I hide a face,
Of pain, anguish and disgrace.
I feel like I could cut my throat and stab my heart
Because I've hated myself from the start.

Other people don't know this pain,
Their efforts to help are all in vain.
It doesn't matter what you say,
I'll hate myself anyway.

Rain, rain, go away,
Is what the kids always say.
When you compare rain to tears,
Depression is one of my biggest fears.

From, me.

Jason Gajari (13)
Brentside High School, London

No One Understands Me

The same routine every day,
All I want to do is stay here all day.
No one understands my wishes,
But when I get home, all I do is the dishes,
Schoolwork, homework,
No time for my own things.
I'm going to carry on tidying my stuff
And stay away from those cuffs.
My parents want me to revise,
But I'm more worried about staying alive.
My parents don't leave me alone,
So all I do is moan.
I'm bored at home,
All I want to do is be alone.

Sarah Smahi (13)
Brentside High School, London

In-Between The Lines

I go back there,
Every now and then.
Places, things, mistakes.
It all happened and yet,
It somehow feels ficticious.

The warm summer days in which you and I played,
The cold ice cream dripping down your face,
The antiseptic which filled my lungs,
The raw stone face.

From the moment I smiled at strangers,
And now when I trip over my feet.
The happy and the sad,
The good and the bad,
It all makes me complete.

Hannah Lunn
Brentside High School, London

Being Small

Being small is really tough,
Especially because the world is rough.
I'm not that tall,
But I can still header a football.
I have to look up at others,
Except for my brothers.

I only want to grow,
Because people just don't know,
What it is like to be small.
I just want to be tall!

Because I'm far too small to go on rides,
Even at the water park I'm bullied by the tides.

Riley Bassoli
Brentside High School, London

Depression

Freak,
Monster,
The names they call me
The devil on my shoulder
The voices in my mind
Worthless,
Pathetic,
The list goes on and on
And whilst my heart is saying, 'Do one thing'
My mind is reeling saying, 'Don't listen to it'
My heart is saying to love
My mind is saying I can't, I never can, I never was and I never will be
But whilst you're there eating what you want, I'm starving myself
Afraid of what you might think if I tell the truth
Afraid you will judge me for battling with things you can't see
Things you can't show
Things you don't even know are there until everything comes crashing down
But I'm afraid
I'm afraid I'll lose this fight
I'm afraid that I'll be loved, but not love back
I'm afraid to be hurt because the scars and burns I bear, are too much to live through again
Too much for a teenager who has nothing to worry about
Too much for a child with a perfect life
Too much for someone who is constantly living in fear of themselves and their mind
I go through this on a daily basis.

So you can sit there, enjoying that low mark you got on that test
Whilst I worry if I can make someone proud when I got ten marks higher
You can sit and enjoy your meals
Whilst I worry about putting on another pound
I drown myself in my fears and worries, and as a border
I use oversized clothes to keep everything in

To stop this thing from leaking everywhere bringing not only me, but everyone else down
And sometimes the blackness is comforting
The thoughts of blood and cuts are so known to me, that I find myself absorbed in a pain that isn't there
In an emotion I cannot feel
So enjoy your time, because I might not be here for long.

Rhianna Mae France (15)
Cockburn School, Leeds

Nature

I look around me,
Beauty is what I see,
But sometimes, I can't see it,
My mind needs to be freed.

I know there is beauty,
Everywhere I look,
But sometimes, I can't see it -
Even though it's an open book.

I know there is beauty,
But at the moment,
I can't see.
Will you sit beside me
Until I see,
The beauty in being free
And
Being
Me?

Jordan Aaron Hardy (14)
Cockburn School, Leeds

The Ghost That Lives Inside Of Me

In the mirror all I see,
Is the ghost that lives inside of me.
The scene is frightening; bloody rags and all,
And it usually carries a blood-red saw.
Every time I'm in the mood to laugh,
It stops that and takes me very far back,
To a swirling state of depression.
It gives me a sense of aggression.
It wants to stay there, I know,
It makes me want to hurt my soul.
In the mirror, all I see
Is the ghost that lives inside of me.

Darren Woodward (12)
Culcheth High School, Warrington

Anguish

They always said we were losers and worthless
They laughed.
They mocked us.
They teased us.

Everything was them.
The plan.
The manslaughter.
The blame.
Even the deceptive role of innocence that they played.
Just because I was there, didn't mean I did it.

It had been building for weeks, they were always after us.
Why couldn't they have just left us alone?
That way no one would have died.

The pain.
The sights and screams of agony were horrific to witness.

After a while there was silence.
Not a single word or breath
Came from the bodies that suffered anguish.

Amar Mohammed
Fullbrook School, Addlestone

The Eternal Woods

Nights come, days go
Birds fly, murder of crows
Through it, something stays
The impending doomsday
Is it Heaven?
Or is it Hell?

What makes the question asked?
What has the present masked?
Who hides in fear
When all wars decide to appear?
Is it soldiers whose fight was shown
Or leaders that stayed at home?
Lives lost for choices made
Are forgotten and never named

The child's tear
His mother, dying near
The father dead
From wars of dread
Single drop
Enough to raise a crop
A crop that rises
To help realise
Life goes on
Through it all.

Diarmait Finch (13)
Ipswich Tuition Centre, Ipswich

My Fantasy Poem

The twinkling fairy dust brushed past my eyes,
All my taste buds started to die.
All I could smell were sugary crumbs,
I looked into the distance and I saw the pink, fluffy clouds.

I opened the latch,
As the breeze went past it picked up the gorgeous smell of golden toffees,
The beautiful sky was starting to get darker and darker.
I was really scared, I looked behind me, guess what I saw?
Coming out of the bushes was a killer clown.

The clown was chasing the train,
But he couldn't run very fast because of his big feet.
Luckily, I took a picture before it was too late,
Loads of policemen came to find him.
From this day I am never going on a train by myself ever again...

Amelie Clarke (11)
Luckley House School, Wokingham

While Dolphins Juggle In The Dining Room

While dolphins juggle in the dining room,
Zebras prance, fly and zoom.
When crocodiles play music loud,
An elephant floats on a cloud.

While giant ants in plastic pants scour the Earth,
Tiny giraffes express their mirth.
When cats and dogs finally make friends,
A hippopotamus is trying new trends.

While slithering snakes drink milkshakes,
Monkeys clear the garden with miniature rakes,
When hedgehogs sharpen their spikes
Lions and sloths go for hikes.

While cows play noughts and crosses,
Ladybugs become bosses,
When leopard spots turn green
Everyone shouts, 'It's Halloween!'

Amelia Shackleford (12)
Samworth Church Academy, Mansfield

It's Time To...

The banjo stopped playing
a sour note in the air
the pulling of his heart,
he knew he had died
The once noisy theatre
was like a sombre play
no boomerang fish were flying
no hecklers in the rafters
no chickens, cows, pigs, koozebanians or frogs
Just friends with friends wishing for the end of the day.
The bear stopped joking
the band stopped playing,
the pig stopped singing.
Instead they talked about the memories
ones they would soon forget.
The service was meant to be quiet
just his friends in arms.
instead they came in force
the children he had helped grow up
tears and songs laid the streets
as they remembered the man he was.
The bear remembered the jokes they shared
the band remembered the songs they played
they all remembered the memories they had made.
Tear-stained fur
and hands gripping tight
they sang his songs
but they were not the same without his voice.
The frog walked up
his frame heavy
the dog followed
feeling lost without his owner
the chef wouldn't cook
the Dr wouldn't play the ivories.
Ernie clung to the rubber duck like a lifeline

What was left for them?
They had lost him
he had lost his life
their life, their movement
in his life he gave them one.
What would they do without their puppeteer?
What would they do without Jim Henson?

Katie Hardwick (15)
Samworth Church Academy, Mansfield

Broken Heart

Whistling wind scratches the window,
From there he watches both of you go,
Laughing happily in sync.
The sound of wine glasses, *clink, clink*,
Cuddled up by the fire,
He stares into your eyes as they tire,
His warmth is love,
His skin as soft as a dove.
He stood there crying in the thunder,
Watching the connection between you and him,
He then began to wander,
Back the other way,
Home again but not happily ever after.

Ellie Carter (11)
Samworth Church Academy, Mansfield

Fears

Eyes stare me down,
not a single sound,
heart beats faster,
shadows lurk around,
nothing can be found.
Why won't it stop?
Your words drown my ears,
laughs cause my fears,
I can hear them calling
As I'm falling,
the light shrouds the darkness,
my fears still live on,
concerns for now are gone,
myself and demons are one.

Tia Southway (12)
Samworth Church Academy, Mansfield

Online

The Internet found me
It didn't leave me
It stayed with me
It haunted me
The keys clicked
The words appeared
The screen grabbed my eyes
Words turned into sentences
Sentences into paragraphs

They grab me
They hit me
They hurt me
They kill me...

Ellie Green (13)
Samworth Church Academy, Mansfield

Appended

Hidden deep in darkness, it lies.
Chasing for years, it thrives.
Revenge it came, it will rise.
I am very much alive.

Stillest approach, it shakes.
Shut the eyes, it wakes.
Make contact, won't escape.
Get out, before it is late.

With its mouth, it will devour.
It has no impact, do not cower.
Finally I break, against the thunder.
Now, I have made an incredible blunder.

Uncalculated, it dives in.
Instantly, the wish to undo my sin.
Deceased, I have been converted as an addition.
Prognosticating, it waits again with ambition.

Laya Kappagantula (13)
Sharp Tutoring, Texas

Young Writers Information

We hope you have enjoyed reading this book – and that you will continue to in the coming years.

If you're a young adult who enjoys reading and creative writing, or the parent of an enthusiastic poet or story writer, do visit our website **www.youngwriters.co.uk**. Here you will find free competitions, workshops and games, as well as recommended reads, a poetry glossary and our blog.

If you would like to order further copies of this book, or any of our other titles, then please give us a call or visit **www.youngwriters.co.uk**.

Young Writers
Remus House
Coltsfoot Drive
Peterborough
PE2 9BF
(01733) 890066
info@youngwriters.co.uk